SEASONED IN THE SOUTH

SEASONED IN THE SOUTH

Recipes from Crook's Corner and from Home

by **BILL SMITH**

ALGONQUIN BOOKS OF CHAPEL HILL 2005

Published by
ALGONQUIN BOOKS OF CHAPEL HILL
Post Office Box 2225
Chapel Hill, North Carolina 27515-2225

a division of
WORKMAN PUBLISHING
708 Broadway
New York, New York 10003

© 2005 by Bill Smith. All rights reserved.
Printed in the United States of America.
Published simultaneously in Canada by Thomas Allen & Son Limited.
Design by Maxine Mills and Anne Winslow.

Grateful acknowledgment for the use of photographs is made to the following: page iii: Kinsley Dey; page x: Mark Wagoner; pages 2 and 3: collection of the author; page 5: Kinsley Dey; page 6: Anne Winslow; page 23: Eric Stern; page 83: Kinsley Dey; pages 134 and 135: Rick Robinson; page 187: Michael Traister.

LIBRARY OF CONGRESS CATALOGING-IN-PUBLICATION DATA
Smith, Bill, 1949 Jan.11–
    Seasoned in the South : recipes and stories from Crook's Corner and from home / Bill Smith.
        p. cm.
    ISBN-13: 978-1-56512-479-0
    ISBN-10: 1-56512-479-0
    1. Cookery, American—Southern style.   2. Crook's Corner (Restaurant)   I. Title.
    TX715.2.S68 S58 2005
    641.5975—dc22   200547814

10 9 8 7 6 5 4 3 2 1
First Edition

To all my cooks. Love and kisses from "the land of blood, meat, and fire."

A todos mis cocineros. Amor y besos desde "la tierra de sangre, carne, y fuego."

CONTENTS

PREFACE

HE FIRST TIME I ever saw Bill Smith he was dancing on top of a table to a song named "Cakewalk to Kansas City" in a show named *Diamond Studs*, a strictly local product created by an outfit known as the Southern States Fidelity Choir. It was summer 1973. Bill wore blue jeans and a red T-shirt and a diamond earring. He was dancing like crazy, and the whole shebang was headed straight to New York.

Looking back, I find this image emblematic of both Bill Smith and Chapel Hill, not only in those wild years when we were all young but today as well. A sleepy little Southern town transformed by a great university, Chapel Hill has always been a haven for artists, writers, and musicians, original thinkers and mavericks of all kinds. Exuberance and innovation flourish. (Back when the North Carolina legislature was discussing whether or not to fund a state zoo, Jesse Helms suggested, "Just put a fence around Chapel Hill.")

No wonder "musicians' theater" originated here or the "new Southern cuisine" was invented at Crook's Corner by Bill Neal and Bill Smith.

Today Bill Smith and Crook's Corner are an institution. You'll find them smack at the center of things, both literally and symbolically.

There's Bill, threading his bike through the traffic on Rosemary Street as he rides to work, greeting everybody along the way, or at the farmers' market every Saturday morning with his basket, choosing kumquats.

And there's the restaurant, right on the corner, in the same building that used to be Miss Rowena Crook's fish market. There it is with its famous Bob Gaston pig sculpture on the roof, along with a lot of Clyde Jones's chain-saw "critters" and a glittery collection of hubcaps on the wall, and big spiky plants and weird flowers growing all over the sidewalk; there it is, looking like a piece of funky folk art itself. It sits right at the intersection of the New South and the Old South. Though Franklin Street has gone corporate a little farther east, Al's Garage is still catty-corner across the street, and gospel music still swells out of the historic St. Paul A.M.E. Church next door.

Inside, Crook's is a combination of a city bistro (black and white tiles on the floor, good art on the walls) and your grandmother's kitchen, with a little bit of New Orleans thrown in. It's almost a party atmosphere.

Though he's a genius cook, Bill Smith is not really a foodie. He's more interested in his diners' total experience: he wants us to enjoy ourselves. Therefore, he is the best host in the world, attentive, expansive, and even exuberant (remember that dancing on the table) in his approach to food.

Bill is wide open to everything. A local Latin American festival inspired his amazing Mango Salad, for instance. His kitchen staff (Vietnamese, East European, Chinese, etc.) has provided many new recipe ideas (as well as great vacations). And since he always cooks from scratch, he invents new dishes on the spot to make use of whatever his longtime farmer friends and suppliers bring him.

He's open to the serendipitous gifts of the season as well. I will never forget one magical midsummer night when my husband and I had just sat down at Crook's; Bill literally bounded up to our table with the news that he had—just that afternoon—created his first Honeysuckle Sorbet after going out to gather the blossoms in the middle of the night, when their perfume is headiest. (This is my second favorite image of Bill.) Another summer favorite of mine is his Tomato and Watermelon Salad; try this, it's unbelievably delicious and refreshing.

Winter brings its comfort food to Crook's: the famous Chicken Pot Pie, soups, stews, roasts, meat loaf. Spring arrives with the best Soft-Shelled Crabs in the world, demystified in these pages. I mean, they are so easy—and if I can make these, you can damn well make them, too.

This is true of all Bill's recipes, by the way. He's never showing off, but he allows us to. So go for it. Try the Cashew Cake and the Really Good Banana Pudding. Jump up on that table! Bill is simplifying for us. So now I can actually cook my absolute all-time favorite dish in the world, Bill's Fried Oysters with Roasted Garlic Mayonnaise. I ate supper at Crook's with my late son every Sunday evening for ten years or so, and I believe we ordered the fried oyster appetizer every time, splitting the generous portion. Now, each bite brings back those treasured evenings. These are happy memories; this is happy food.

—Lee Smith

SEASONED IN THE SOUTH

INTRODUCTION

Cuisines de Grand-mère and Grandmother

I REMEMBER THE FIRST TIME I ever cooked anything amandine. It was the late 1960s. We lived in big group houses. I had just bought my first color TV and Julia Child preceded *Masterpiece Theatre* on Sunday nights on PBS. We would cook whatever she said and then sit down to eat and to watch *Thérèse Raquin* or *The Moonstone*. We felt like we were leading very civilized lives indeed. It would be many years before I would cook for a living. I first had to work on my checkered past.

My first serious kitchen job was a part-time position. I was planning to travel to Europe with a friend and I needed extra cash. One of my roommates was the head waitress at a French restaurant, and the kitchen there needed someone to peel potatoes and chop parsley. When I came back that fall, the job was still there. The aesthetic of cooking had suited me to a tee, but I had never considered it as a profession. My luck is such that I often fall into good situations unaware.

Restaurant kitchens are places of attrition, and within five years or so I found myself promoted to head chef. The restaurant was a small upscale place with an eye toward the traditional *cuisine bourgeoise*, that everyday yet refined cooking of the middle class. We did all the classics: beef burgundy, coq au vin, tart Tatin, etc. This was not such a great cultural leap for me given my grandmothers.

I grew up at a time and in a family where good meals together were a matter of course, understood to be essential. I come from sturdy Southern middle-class stock, and Southerners share more with the French than just New Orleans. Sensibilities can be similar as well. I grew up being cooked for by relatives who had survived the Depression but who still expected food to be good in spite of the privation. The *cuisine de grand-mère* that we practiced at La Residence was similarly formed at the same place — where the expectation of good food collides with the need for economy. That was the cuisine of my *grand-mère* as well. It was a key element in a calm, modest, and orderly home.

Aunt Hi

THE KITCHEN IN my father's mother's house was presided over by my Aunt Hi, a wonderful cook who was never satisfied unless you left the Sunday dinner table in a gluttonous stupor. In my mother's mother's house the kitchen's overseer was my great-grandmother Inez, remarkable for both her cooking and for the age at which she continued to do it.

Every weekday she prepared an enormous midday meal for everyone in the extended family who had "put their name in the pot." In those days in the South, big lunches and lighter suppers were still the custom. These lunches were always called dinner and we all would come from school and office whenever we could.

Both of these women cooked Southern after their own fashion. Hi was from Georgia and her cooking was more traditional. Chicken with pastry comes to mind. Grandmother had Northerners as grandparents—"those mean Yankee Germans," everyone

My great-grandmother (left)

called them—and sometimes their cuisine would infiltrate, albeit informed by a generation in North Carolina. She often cooked lamb, which was unusual. I was absolutely raised on sauerkraut and for years I ate tripe sautéed in butter and bread crumbs because I had been told it was fish.

I began chefing in the late 1970s, just when new American cuisine was beginning its roll and nouvelle cuisine had reared its head in France. We anticipated the publication of certain cookbooks like others did blockbuster movies. A parade of new ingredients began appearing in cooking magazines and we would send emissaries to big cities to bring them back. Pesto, kiwis, pink peppercorns, sun-dried tomatoes, and balsamic vinegar all took their turns.

Sometime during the ensuing twenty-five years, something strange has happened. We went from demanding that women be allowed to have careers outside of the home to needing wives to work as well as husbands. So now when I see the wonder that a plain-roasted chicken can produce, I realize that almost no one cooks regularly anymore. People have no time. Cooking today often seems to be either a hobby or a nerve-racking project such as preparing a big dinner party or a traditional holiday meal. I doubt that this is going to change anytime soon, and so I've tried to make this book a reliable, easy-to-follow, and hopefully entertaining project guide that might also be of interest to the hobbyists.

I've simplified my approach to food over the years and most of these recipes reflect that. In the heady 1970s I sought out the rococo; now I prefer meals that are to be eaten and not dissected at the table—good food as a backdrop for good conversation.

I've tried to arrange these recipes in a logical way, but that doesn't always work. Sometimes the order of preparation isn't the same as the order of presentation.

The recipes do follow what I see as a logical seasonal progression: a year in the kitchen. This is the way I direct my menu. The weather, the farmer, and the fisherman dictate it as much as I do. This rule makes good cooking easy and continually provides favorite things to look forward to year after year.

Over the years, almost without noticing it, I've gathered a network of local people who supply me with much of my produce, seafood, and dairy. If you try to do as much from scratch as possible, then this enforces seasonality on your menu. It also keeps your money in the community and strikes a tiny blow against corporate agriculture and the mass-market food industry. Best of all it's always, always better.

This all started years ago when Mrs. Mary Andrews called me up out of the blue to see if I would buy one hundred stems of mint for six dollars. Fourteen years later I'm still buying from her, as well as from her sister and some of their friends. I've known Ken Dawson, from whom I buy produce, since 1968, long before I was a cook and just when he was beginning to farm. I've known Cathy Jones almost that long. I get a wonderfully refined herby salad mix from her.

Some of the people I buy from now I see at the farmers' market, but most of them I deal with directly through phone ordering. I use my vis-

its to the market to fine-tune the menu. I might find pretty herbs or unusual vegetables. Often there are nice radishes for the pâté plate or tomatoes for a summer salad. I can also buy flowers for the bar.

Wonderful cheese is made here now, and produce like fennel and exotic chile peppers are grown in bulk, but my real treasure may be the farmers who just grow a little of this and that from time to time and who call me when they think about it. It is from them that I get things like fresh figs, Jerusalem artichokes, mayhaws, Kieffer pears, persimmons, a couple cups of raspberries, or a few bunches of baby turnips. Oh, and the pounds and pounds of shelled pecan halves . . .

THERE ARE A LOT of recipes from the restaurant kitchen repertoire that are impossible to pass on because they depend on an ongoing ac-

cumulation of scraps and leftovers that would not be found in the home. Once upon a time I suspect that the kitchens of large, multigenerational families worked like this, but those days are gone. To me, the good use of these things is almost a point of honor. This probably comes from being raised by people who survived the Depression. It seems wrong to be wasteful. To my staff, I probably just appear cheap.

My recipe tester and I chuckled as we contemplated instructions that begin, "Take some old, dry this" or "Save the membranes, drippings, and cartilage from that," but many of these things add extra layers of flavor and nuance that would be otherwise impossible. A handful of fresh herb stems is always welcome in the stock pot, as are the skins, seeds, and juice of fresh tomatoes that have been diced for dressings and garnish. Stale garlic toast is an excellent thickener for certain soups or as a base for aioli. Bones are invaluable for stocks and sauces. Fresh pork fat is priceless for terrines and pâtés. We clarify gallons of butter for sautéing. The discarded curds and whey make spectacular risotto. We generate gallons of egg whites. These become macaroons, nut tortes, and meringues. We sift nuts before toasting them because the small crumbs will burn. The siftings can be incorporated into cookie dough. The trimmings from puff pastry become wonderful little cookies for ice creams.

I save chicken and duck livers in the freezer one by one until I have enough for a pâté. Ditto for the little crumbs of sweetbreads that are too small to use in a main course. We also trim lots of beef. All of the scraps are browned in the oven and added to the stock pot. Pork shoulders become a Sunday night pot roast. Ham bones, scraps, and fats become seasonings for collards and black-eyed peas. Parmesan cheese rinds can be added to vegetable stocks if you are careful—they want to sink and scorch. And mushrooms that have darkened a little past prime make the best mushroom soup.

Last but not least, pork ribs roasted to a crisp with lots of salt and pepper, and duck hearts and gizzards rescued from the roasting pan, make excellent snacks for the staff.

All this reminiscing makes me realize how long I've been at this and I find it startling. I owe a great debt to all of my colleagues and coworkers of the last twenty-five years. The profession and those people have added an amusing layer of richness to my life that I doubt I could have found anywhere else, other than in a hot kitchen.

FALL

IT'S ABOUT TEN BLOCKS to work and I always ride my bike. As I round the corner at Pritchard and Rosemary, I catch the first aroma. Brown sauce at La Residence where I once worked. A block further along the bistro is caramelizing onions. At Mediterranean Deli they are making *mujaderra*. Then a cluster of Asian places with the smells of sesame oil and curry. If the breeze is right, there will be the fragrance of one of those wonderful stews from the Ethiopian restaurant. Recently, the aroma of *pho* has arrived at the corner of Church and Franklin streets. As you might guess, there is a sort of restaurant district on the west side of Chapel Hill. In the fall there is something about cool, damp weather that causes smells to linger in the air. I first noticed this years ago when I lived in New York and would walk by the chestnut and hot dog carts.

Chapel Hill is a university town, and our year really begins in the fall. North Carolina is often still mild at this time of year, so there is more likely to be a slow decline in local produce rather than an abrupt ending caused by a sudden freeze. In mid-October I get my last bag of salad herbs from Cathy Jones. It changes as the summer progresses; the final batch is usually heavy on kales and arugula with a sprinkling of marigold petals and basil tips. The cheese makers keep going until Christmas week. Mrs. Andrews brings me her last persimmons. Between the rain and the deer she says there aren't many left. Her sister Blanche Norwood should have plenty of pecans, though. Bill Dow will soon have fennel again, one of our best cool weather crops, which ten years ago had to be special-ordered from California. We find ourselves entering the season of bulbs, roots, and stews, much of which will call for good stocks.

STOCKS

IN MY KITCHEN there is almost always a stockpot on the stove. Stocks are the real foundation of good cooking. Even if you are really busy and need to find shortcuts, I would still advise taking the time to make stock. Generally, I use either a brown stock or a poultry stock, but I am something of a medievalist in this regard and will pitch pork bones into the chicken stock or chicken carcasses into the veal broth if I have them.

BROWN STOCK

Brown stock is the basis for Bourbon Brown Sauce (page 171), which I use in many ways. Almost no one goes to the trouble of making this from scratch anymore. I've always been proud of the fact that we do at Crook's Corner. It's hard to make a small amount of this successfully, but it can be reduced to a syrup by boiling and can be frozen for later use.

Makes about 1 gallon

8 pounds veal (or beef if you must) bones

2 large carrots, peeled and sliced (about two cups)

2 large onions, peeled and coarsely chopped (about four cups)

1 bunch celery, leaves discarded, washed and chopped (about four cups)

1½ cups dry red wine

3 bay leaves

1 tablespoon whole black peppercorns

In cool weather, 1 turnip, peeled and chopped (optional)

Other meat and vegetable scraps

Cool water

Preheat the oven to 375° F. Spread the bones evenly on a sheet pan and roast until they are a pretty reddish brown color all over. It will be necessary to rotate the pan and turn the bones often to prevent burning. This will take at least an hour depending on the oven and the size and moisture content of the bones. In the restaurant I almost always have meat scraps (generally pork or beef) left over from butchering, and I put these onto the pan as well. (Poultry is okay, but beware of lamb because of its strong flavor.) This boosts the meatiness of the stock. Some people like to brown the vegetables as well, but I rarely do.

Put the browned bones in the stockpot, discarding anything that has burned or blackened because it will make the stock bitter. Then you must deglaze the pan. This means setting it on top of the stove over the highest heat and pouring on the wine to dissolve all the cooked-on bits of meat and juice. Use a spatula to dislodge everything and scrape all of it into the pot. Fill the pot with cool water and the rest of the red wine. Then add the carrots, onions, celery, bay leaves, and peppercorns. In winter I add a turnip to the stock, but only one because its flavor is so strong. This is a habit I picked up years ago in Quebec where it is common. It will give the stock a sturdier finish for the cold weather.

I simmer this stock very slowly over low heat for at least 3 days. Most people I know won't have the nerve to do this at home, but I recommend cooking this for as long as possible. Put it on early in the morning when you will be home all day. In the restaurant we continually produce vegetable scraps that will improve the stock, and I pitch these in during the entire cooking process. The peels and seeds of tomatoes are particularly good additions. You have to be careful, however, not to add so much stuff that there is not enough liquid. If the stockpot is easy to stir, you should be okay. Resist the temptation to add salt since in all likelihood the stock will be reduced later, magnifying its saltiness.

When the stock is rich and tasty, strain and degrease it. Use in making Bourbon Brown Sauce for Grilled Steaks and Sautéed Chicken Livers (page 171).

CHICKEN STOCK

This is a slightly different way to produce a good chicken stock. Whole chickens are poached in a method that the Chinese call velvetizing. The meat can be used in another recipe such as Millionaires' Chicken (page 168), but because the recipe begins with raw chicken the cook must go hungry initially.

Makes about 4 quarts

2 whole chickens (about 3 pounds each), well rinsed and patted dry
1 large carrot, peeled and chopped (about 1 cup)
3 stalks celery, leaves discarded, washed and chopped (about 1 cup)
1 large onion, peeled and chopped (about 2 cups)
Water
1 teaspoon salt (optional)

In a large stockpot, bring to a boil enough water (about 6 quarts) to float the two chickens. Add the chickens. When the boil returns, set a timer for 15 minutes. At the end of that time turn off the heat, cover the stockpot, and let sit for 20 minutes. Then remove the chickens from the broth and refrigerate. Return the stock to a boil. As soon as the chickens are cool enough, pick the meat from the carcasses and reserve it for another recipe. Add the skin and bones back into the stock along with the vegetables. If the broth will be used for soup, add the salt now. If the broth is for sauce, don't. Simmer until the bones fall apart, about 40 minutes more. Strain and degrease the stock.

DUCK STOCK

No matter which part of the duck I plan to use, the first thing I do is to prepare a stock. I always brown the carcasses, although there are certain Asian recipes that call for the duck to be used raw.

Makes about 4 quarts

Duck bones and giblets, minus the livers, from 2 whole ducks

1½ cups of dry white or red wine

2 large onions, peeled and chopped

1 head celery, leaves discarded, washed and chopped

2 large carrots, peeled and chopped

2 bay leaves

1 teaspoon whole black peppercorns

Cool water

Preheat the oven to 350° F. Place the bones and giblets out on a sheet pan, spreading them as far apart as you can, and cook until they are a pretty dark red color, at least 45 minutes. Discard anything that appears burned or the stock will taste bitter. Turn them from time to time as they cook. Although I cook all the hearts and gizzards this way, they rarely make it into the stockpot because I can't resist rolling them in salt and pepper and eating them right out of the oven. I'm the only person I know who can reach into the cavity of a dead bird, withdraw a handful of entrails, and consider himself lucky. If I nibble at all, I know I'm doomed, so sometimes I quickly put everything into the stockpot to remove the temptation. Gizzards floating in cold water are not as appetizing.

Deglaze the roasting pan with the wine. I can never decide whether I prefer red or white for this. I just grab what's handy. Put the bones and the deglazing liquid into the pot and cover with water. Add the vegetables, bay leaves, and peppercorns, and simmer over moderate heat until the carcasses have fallen completely apart and the stock has begun to smell like delicious soup, at least 3 hours. Strain and degrease. Use for Duck and Onion Soup (page 40) or in a sauce for Seared Duck Breast (page 49).

JERUSALEM ARTICHOKE RELISH

JERUSALEM ARTICHOKES ARE actually my father's forte. He makes both pickles and relish, and I've eaten them all my life. They are not artichokes at all but the root of a perennial native sunflower. Lots of people used to grow them, but this is no longer the case. They are harder to find every year. I've been getting them from my friend Mary Andrews for a long time, but recent droughts have made them scarcer yet. They can be very dirty because of their irregular shape, with hidden pockets of clumped dirt. However, almost everyone says that if you get them too clean, they don't taste right. Mrs. Andrews puts hers in a hosiery bag and washes them on the gentle cycle of her washing machine in cold water.

Jerusalem artichokes have an addictive quality. My hometown of New Bern, North Carolina, abounds with tales of people who pester my father all fall for jars of the stuff. When the gift arrives, they rush off to a back room or a garage and quickly gobble down the whole thing before anyone else can have any.

I usually make this in twenty-pound batches, which isn't as much as it sounds, especially if you are planning to can it for gifts.

Makes 8 pints

5 pounds of Jerusalem artichokes, washed and trimmed of blemishes

1 quart apple cider vinegar

2 cups sugar

2 teaspoons salt

2 tablespoons turmeric

4 teaspoons dry mustard

1 large onion, peeled, halved, and thinly sliced

1 large bell pepper (any color), cored, seeded, and thinly sliced

1½ teaspoons whole mustard seeds

1½ teaspoons whole celery seeds

A few bay leaves

Grate the Jerusalem artichokes in a food processor using the coarsest disk. Bring the vinegar, sugar, salt, turmeric, and dried mustard to a full boil in a large nonreactive pot that is big enough to comfortably hold all the vegetables as well. Stir occasionally to help dissolve the sugar. Add the onion and pepper, and return to a boil. Add the artichokes. Bring this back to a boil once again and cook it for only 10 minutes more. You want the relish to retain some crunch. Add the mustard seed, celery seed, and bay leaves. The relish keeps well in the refrigerator and can also be canned using sealing jars and a water bath.

I have always loved pickles with meat, so I like to put this on a grilled steak that has been painted with a little brown sauce (see page 171). It is also great on hamburgers.

FRIED FISH WITH GREEN TOMATO RELISH

MY FRIEND LESLIE Jackson gave me the recipe for this relish years ago, so many years ago that it probably bears no resemblance to the original now. She got it from her mother in Baton Rouge. The only thing I remember are these instructions: "Bring back to the boil. Stir from the bottom up with a long spoon. *Cook for fifteen minutes only!*" I always do this.

I used to use this relish as a garnish for white beans or any kind of bean soup, but I have lately discovered it to be a splendid sauce for fried fish fillets. I am partial to bluefish, which has two seasons on the North Carolina coast. You may use any kind of fish you like.

> 1 cup all-purpose flour
>
> 1 teaspoon salt
>
> ½ teaspoon freshly ground black pepper
>
> 4 bluefish fillets (about 6 ounces each), rinsed and patted dry
>
> 4 tablespoons (½ stick) unsalted clarified butter or cooking oil
>
> 1½ cups Green Tomato Relish (page 21)

Season the flour with the salt and pepper. Dredge the fillets in the flour and shake off the excess. Heat the butter or oil in a medium skillet until it sizzles if you sprinkle a little of the flour into it. Add the fish, being careful not to crowd it. Cook, turning once, 2–3 minutes per side depending on the thickness and type of the fish. Bluefish tends to be moist and dense and will take the full 3 minutes, whereas something like flounder, which is thin and dry, will require less time per side. When the fish is done, remove it to a serving platter and pour off the grease, saving any brown bits that might be in the pan.

Add the relish to the pan and bring to a boil. Allow the liquid in the relish to reduce a tiny bit, about 2 minutes to thicken the sauce. Pour over the fish and serve at once.

GREEN TOMATO RELISH

Green tomatoes are available at different times for different reasons. If you have a late crop and frost threatens, you may have to pick everything on one night. Some people like to thin their tomato crop by picking some while green so that the remaining ones will be larger and better. The tomatoes one finds in the grocery store in winter might as well be green.

Makes 10 cups

2 cups apple cider vinegar

1 cup sugar

1½ teaspoons whole allspice berries

1½ teaspoons whole celery seeds

2 or 3 bay leaves

2 large red bell peppers, cored, seeded, and cut into strips

2 large yellow onions, peeled and cut into strips

5 pounds green tomatoes, washed, hulled, and cut into 6 wedges

In a large nonreactive stainless steel or enamel pot, bring the apple cider vinegar to a boil. Add the sugar and stir until it dissolves. Then add the allspice berries, celery seeds, bay leaves, bell peppers, and onions. Bring back to the boil and cook for 15 minutes. Finally, add the tomato wedges and cook for 15 minutes only. This relish may be put up in Mason jars, but it keeps very well in the refrigerator for as long as two months.

Jimmy Carter's Favorite Chaser

I can't bring myself to drink buttermilk. I like it fine in recipes, but the thought of drinking a whole glass of it plain is over the top. I keep expecting to grow into it someday, the way I did with kidneys and anchovies, but I don't think that this is going to happen. Some people, however, actually ask for buttermilk, usually at the end of their meal.

Jimmy Carter is one of those people. He first came to Crook's Corner in 1997. He had a granddaughter studying at Duke University down the road, and came for dinner once when he and Mrs. Carter were visiting. The Secret Service came a week in advance to approve the premises. We don't like to draw attention to famous people who come to eat with us, but of course by the day of the visit everyone in town knew who would be coming to dinner and all the other tables in the restaurant were booked.

The Carters arrived in the middle of the dinner hour and were seated in a back corner. The place was full but no one bothered them. I stayed in the kitchen with my staff, but hoped that I would get to meet the president before he left. Suddenly he walked through my kitchen door. He'd wanted to meet the people who had made his dinner.

My staff that night were almost all from Mexico. I introduced him and he greeted them in Spanish, and then in English he asked me to tell them that he hoped that their experiences in this country had been positive. We talked about the election monitoring that the

Carter Center was about to conduct in Eritrea, and then he returned to his table and asked for a glass of buttermilk. Happily, I always have some on hand—not to drink, but for cornbread and fried chicken batter.

When they got up to leave, the whole restaurant, as if on cue, was suddenly on its feet applauding. It was remarkable.

Several years later, the Carters returned, when a grandson—another student at Duke—held his rehearsal dinner at the restaurant. The president brought me an inscribed copy of his memoir, *The Hour before Daylight*. I couldn't believe that he had remembered me. I had remembered that Mrs. Carter liked liver, so I had made her a little chicken liver terrine. They seemed equally amazed at my memory.

PORK COUNTRY PÂTÉ

ONE BENEFIT OF dressing your own meat is that you can use the trimmings to make pâté. There is no real recipe for pâté because you use whatever you have in whatever amounts you have it. Pâté is clearly the invention of that clever *grand-mère* who wanted to use what would otherwise go to waste. However, there are a few rules that are better followed than ignored. The ratio of fat to lean should be about one-quarter to three-quarters. Slow cooking is essential, and it is better to cook a pâté a day in advance so it can cool thoroughly and set up better for unmolding and slicing.

Everything else is negotiable. I have a heavy, porcelain-coated cast-iron terrine at home to cook pâtés in, but a loaf pan will do if you are careful about not overcooking. I line the terrine with caul fat (the lacy fat that lines the organ cavity of pigs—ask your butcher) if I have it, but bacon or thinly sliced fresh pork fat trimmings will also work. Smoked bacon will add a smoky flavor to the pâté. Because I butcher whole pork loins, I almost always have whole tenderloins on hand, so I roll them in black pepper and bury them down the center of the loaf. My technique is somewhat French, although I don't remember how or from whom I learned it.

My terrine holds about three pounds of pâté, so this recipe is based on that amount. You should be able to buy ground pork at most meat departments.

Makes one 3-pound pâté

12–16 ounces caul fat, or tissue-thin sliced bacon or side meat

1 cup cubed stale bread

2 egg whites beaten into a ½ cup heavy cream

1 generous tablespoon salt

1 tablespoon bacon grease

3 pounds pork ground up like hamburger

1 teaspoon dried thyme

1 teaspoon five-spice powder

⅛ teaspoon of dried red pepper flakes

¼ teaspoon of freshly ground nutmeg

¼ cup raw shelled pistachios

½ cup blanched spinach, wrung dry and coarsely chopped, or 1 cup
   frozen spinach, thawed and squeezed dry

3 bay leaves

Preheat the oven to 350° F. Line a 9 × 5-inch loaf pan or pâté terrine with the fat or bacon. Soak the stale bread (at work I use old garlic toast) in the egg whites and cream mixture until completely soggy. Mix the bread and its liquid, the salt, and the bacon grease into the pork. You have to use your hands. Make a small patty of this and fry it until cooked through. Taste for salt. There is no reason to go to all this trouble if your end product is underseasoned; pâté is never going to be a health food anyway, so you should go for the most delicious result possible. If your pâté is salty enough, add the thyme, five-spice powder, pepper flakes, nutmeg, pistachios, and spinach, and mix thoroughly. Fill the lined terrine and press down firmly to remove any air space. It's okay if the pork piles up higher than the sides of the pan. Cover the top with more caul fat, fresh fat, or bacon. Lay the bay leaves on this and then cover the top with plastic wrap. (It won't melt; this is one of the kitchen mysteries, like the formation of mayonnaise.) My pan has a lid so I put it over the plastic. If you have no lid, cover tightly with foil. Bake in a pan of simmering water about 2 inches deep for 1½ hours, or until a thermometer at the center of the loaf registers 150° F.

When it's done, remove from the oven and take off the lid or foil. Pour out the water from the baking, but leave the pâté in the pan. Place a weight on the pâté. A clean brick wrapped in plastic wrap is perfect. A similar-sized pan with a heavy can in it will also do. The weight will cause the juices to run over, so cool the pâté in its baking pan. Refrigerate overnight. The juices will congeal in the pan, and if there are enough of them, the aspic can be used for garnish.

To unmold the pâté, place the terrine in a pan of warm water for a few minutes. This will melt the fat around the outside and allow you to pop the pâté out of its mold easily. When slicing, use rapid back-and-forth motions rather than pressing straight down with the knife. The pate will have a pretty polished appearance. Serve with pickles, mustard, some kind of toast or cracker, the pâté's aspic cut into small cubes, and Onion Jam (page 29).

TWO- (OR THREE-) BIRD PÂTÉ

As PÂTÉS GO, this one is fairly quick and easy. It is also very messy. I use a standard pâté terrine — a heavy-duty loaf pan that holds around six cups — which I line with buttered parchment. (A 9 × 5-inch loaf pan will also work.) For this pan I use three pounds of chicken (and/or duck) livers. You will also need a sieve and either a food processor or a food mill, although forcing raw livers through a food mill is gruesome business.

Makes one 3-pound pâté

2 tablespoons of butter, softened to room temperature

2 large shallots, peeled and minced

1 tablespoon bacon grease

1 jigger of Wild Turkey bourbon plus a few drops more

3 pounds poultry livers (chicken, duck, or both)

1 large egg

2 egg yolks

1 generous tablespoon salt

¼ teaspoon freshly grated nutmeg

3 drops Tabasco or other hot pepper sauce

3 drops freshly squeezed lemon juice

3 or 4 bay leaves or fresh sage leaves

Preheat oven to 350° F. Butter the pâté pan, line it with kitchen parchment, and then butter the parchment. Place a shallow baking pan larger than your terrine in the oven.

Sauté the shallots in the bacon grease until wilted but not brown, about 5 minutes. As soon as they are done, add the jigger of Wild Turkey (this is one of the birds), being careful, as it will flare up. I usually move the pan away from the flame, add the whiskey, and then return to the flame to ignite it. Swirl the pan until the alcohol is burned off. Remove from heat, add a few drops of fresh whiskey, and allow the shallots to cool.

Meanwhile, place the livers in the food processor and grind. Add the egg and egg yolks, salt, nutmeg, Tabasco, lemon juice, and the cooled shallots. This can be really messy, so you might want to grind it in two batches. (I have an uncanny ability to splash this into my eye.) Strain the livers through a sieve or food mill and fill the lined terrine. It will be very much like a batter. Float the bay or sage leaves on top. Then cover very tightly with plastic wrap.

Fill the baking pan under the terrine with hot water and bake for 45 minutes, or until the pâté appears firm at the center. Remove the plastic wrap and cook until the top has begun to brown and the internal temperature has reached 150° F but no more, about 10 minutes. A knife blade inserted into the center should come out clean. Sometimes the top will crack, but that's okay. Cool completely (it's preferable to refrigerate overnight). To unmold, place the pan in warm water for a few minutes.

Years ago, my boss, the late Bill Neal, made me taste a liver terrine before it was cooked to make sure that it had enough salt. I expected to choke, but instead I discovered that if you like liver, you *really* like raw liver. Of course, today, I would never eat raw liver, but I feel like I have gone over one of those thresholds better left uncrossed.

ONION JAM

I USE SLOW-COOKED ONIONS for a variety of dishes. The longer and slower they cook the better. For this reason, onion jam is a good project for a day spent at home. I make this in an old dutch oven with a heavy lid. This recipe makes about a quart, but a large batch is an excellent project for a homemade holiday gift, and you can be reasonably sure that you will be the only one giving it. I've used it for years on pâté plates, but it is also good with ham and on grilled strip steaks or a London broil.

Makes 1 quart

4 tablespoons (½ stick) unsalted butter

5 pounds yellow onions, peeled, halved, and thinly sliced

¾ cup sugar

1 cup red wine vinegar

1 cup dry red wine

¼ cup grenadine syrup

1½ teaspoon freshly ground black pepper

Melt 2 tablespoons of the butter in a heavy-bottomed pot with a tight-fitting lid. Add as many of the onions as you can. You may have to add them in batches, waiting each time for the previous ones to collapse. It is best to wilt the onions for a long time before adding other ingredients. I weight down the pot lid with a cast-iron skillet to help trap the steam inside. After 10 minutes or so, you will discover that the onions are swimming in their own juice. Simmer them for as long as you can, but at least for 30 minutes, before continuing.

Pour the sugar over the onions and wash it down with the vinegar. Again, let this simmer, covered, for as long as you can but at least long enough to dissolve all of the sugar, 5 minutes minimum. The liquid will now begin to reduce back down. When it begins to thicken, uncover and turn up the heat, but be careful not to brown the onions or caramelize the sugar. Add the red wine. Begin stirring constantly. You want the jam to become as thick as possible without browning or, more likely, scorching. You need to stop doing anything else at this point. When you've reduced the jam as much as you dare, about 20 minutes, add the grenadine, stir briskly, and bring back to a boil for a second or two. Stir in the pepper and the remaining 2 tablespoons of the butter.

This keeps very well in the refrigerator almost indefinitely, but you can put it up in jars following the same procedures that your canner recommends for jams and jellies.

This recipe calls for grenadine, which used to be a fruit syrup made from pomegranates, but I very much doubt that the glittering red stuff that we buy today bears any resemblance to the original. It does, however, impart a pretty red hue to the jam. I have discovered lately that Middle Eastern stores have something called pomegranate *melasse*, or molasses, which is probably closer to the original. It tastes better, but since it is almost black it is not as pretty.

FRIED OYSTERS WITH ROASTED GARLIC MAYONNAISE

YOU CAN BUY OYSTERS all year round, but I am old-fashioned and prefer to use them during the cooler months. Oysters pulled out of warm water in hot weather don't seem as appealing. They also seem less safe, although my father says that old-timers down east said it was impossible to eat a bad oyster because it comes right back up. Most people don't realize that seafood is just as seasonal as agriculture, so the fisherman dictates my menu just as surely as the farmer. Most of my seafood comes from the North Carolina coast and we follow its rhythms.

People go wild for these oysters. The secret is corn flour in the breading, not cornmeal. This is used to make tortillas and the like in Mexico. The difference is remarkable. Recently, my local *tienda* was out of regular corn flour and I had to buy Maseca, which is milled for making tamales. This is the best yet.

Serves 4

2 cups Maseca instant corn masa mix

2 teaspoons salt

1 teaspoon freshly ground black pepper

1 cup self-rising flour

1 pint shucked oysters

2 cups Canola or peanut oil for frying the oysters

Coarse sea salt

Roasted Garlic Mayonnaise (page 32)

Mix the Maseca, salt, pepper, flour. Taste the dredge to make sure that it is seasoned well enough for you. Drain the oysters a little at a time by shaking them in a skeleton spoon. Toss them in the breading. Shake off the excess and fry in uncrowded batches in the hot (365°F on a candy thermometer) oil. If you don't have a candy thermometer, wait until the oil begins to shimmer and then sprinkle a little of the breading into it. It should sizzle vigorously. The oil should be deep enough to float the oysters. Let the oil recover its heat between each batch. The oysters only need to cook for a minute to a minute and a half, until they are just beginning to brown. Drain them on a clean kitchen towel, toss with the coarse sea salt, and serve at once with Roasted Garlic Mayonnaise.

ROASTED GARLIC MAYONNAISE

When I was growing up it was generally understood that under no circumstances should you eat garlic if you were going out in public. Smelling of garlic was considered untidy at best and unpleasantly ethnic at worst. I once found a Spanish phrase book that listed "no garlic, please" among its useful entries. Later, when I actually went to Spain, I was warned that it was nice but that everything smelled of garlic. I found Spain delightful. Southerners in particular think that everyone ought to smell like the Avon lady, but when I shifted from a French to a Southern restaurant, I decided that this was one place where I would have to break form. I never ever shy away from garlic.

Roasted garlic mayonnaise is good with lots of things but foremost with fried oysters. Once upon a time I would have made mayonnaise from scratch (and might still in my home), but fear of new strains of egg-borne salmonellas keeps me from serving raw eggs to the public, and now I use Hellmann's. I must say, though, that it is hard to imagine any microbes surviving in all this garlic. I prefer the rougher extra-virgin olive oils that are found in Greek and Middle Eastern grocery stores.

Makes 3 generous cups

5 plump heads fresh garlic

1 tablespoon extra-virgin olive oil

2 teaspoons whole cumin seeds

3 cups mayonnaise

1 tablespoon freshly squeezed lemon juice

1 tablespoon onion powder

1 teaspoon sugar (optional)

Salt to taste

Preheat the oven to 350° F. Toss the garlic in the oil to just moisten it and then add in the cumin seeds and the salt. Transfer to a small baking dish with a lid (an envelope of tightly sealed aluminum foil also works great for this) and roast tightly covered for 1½ hours. You don't want any of the steam to escape. The garlic should be soft and aromatic and have just begun to ooze delicious, sticky caramel-colored syrup.

Allow the garlic to cool enough to handle, but remember that the next step will be easier if the garlic is a little warm. Different members of my staff have different preferences for ways to get the garlic out of its husk, but whatever you do you are in for a sticky mess. I don latex gloves, pull out the hard root from the bottom of each bulb, and squeeze the garlic into a food mill. Pureeing will remove any peel that may have escaped you as well as incorporate more of the cumin seeds. Fold the puree into the mayonnaise, and then add the lemon juice and onion powder. Taste, and season accordingly. If the garlic isn't sweet enough, add sugar. You may also decide that you like more lemon juice. Add some salt, but remember that the mayonnaise will already have some.

Serve as a dip for fried oysters. People also often ask for this with their french fries.

MUSSELS WITH SAFFRON

MUSSELS AND SAFFRON are one of those almost eerie flavor combinations that really belong together. Everyone has his or her own list of these. Mine includes tomatoes and basil, of course, and sesame oil with soy sauce, but also things like chicken with leeks, cumin and red beans, and chocolate and raspberries.

Saffron is decidedly exotic. My grandmother was a good cook and a skilled gardener. Perhaps because of this she was fascinated by saffron—the stamen of a fall blooming crocus that is used as a seasoning. She had a vial of it on her spice rack that we were allowed to admire, but as far as I remember it was never used. This would have been in the early 1960s and none of us could believe that such a tiny speck of it cost seven dollars.

This recipe is an old favorite, very easy and quite elegant. I like to use lots of mussels—3 cups per person at least.

Serves 4–6

1 pound fettuccini

6 large shallots, peeled and finely chopped (about 1½ cups)

1½ dry white wine

3 cups heavy cream

½ teaspoon saffron

3–4 pounds live, cleaned mussels in their shells,
    scrubbed and beard removed

Cook the fettuccini according to the instructions on the package. Put the shallots in a large saucepan with a tight-fitting lid. Add the wine and reduce over high heat until almost dry (about 5 minutes). Try not to brown the shallots around the edge of the pan. Add the cream and the saffron.

Reduce this sauce over medium heat (it will want to boil over) until it is bright yellow and a little bit viscous, about 10 minutes, depending on the cream. Bring to a hard boil, quickly add the mussels, and cover for a moment. Bring it back to a simmer and cook only until the mussels begin to just open. They will have emitted a lot of their own juice at this point, so quickly remove them to their serving dish and crank up the heat under the sauce to reduce it back down some. Add the cooked fettuccini and toss to coat. Pour the sauce (and pasta) over the mussels and serve at once. A plain green salad completes a splendid supper.

HI'S OYSTER STEW

MY AUNT HI (née Ensel Highsmith) was married to my father's only brother. She came from the coast of Georgia and was a wonderful cook. For many years I would go to her house for Sunday dinner (as lunch was called in those days). You were expected to eat yourself into a stupor. Hi beamed as you took seconds and thirds of everything. It was often necessary to lie down after one of these meals. Remarkably, I was a very skinny child. My mother tells me, though I don't remember, that when I was little I would help Hi when she baked pies. Perhaps that was the beginning of my trek to the professional kitchen. I associate this oyster stew recipe with Hi, but it is widely used all over eastern North Carolina. It can be a soup, a main course, and is very often used as food for the sick room.

Serves 4–6

1 quart whole milk

30–40 shucked oysters with their liquor

1 teaspoon salt

1½ teaspoons freshly ground black pepper

3 tablespoons unsalted butter

1 bunch scallions (white and green parts), trimmed and sliced (optional)

Saltines or oyster crackers

Bring the milk to a boil over medium-high heat in a large nonreactive pan. Add the oysters and their liquor, and bring back to a low simmer. The oysters should barely begin to curl around the edges to be done, a minute at most. Season with salt and pepper. Put the butter in the bottom of each bowl and fill with the hot soup. This is a simple soup and it needn't be tampered with, but some people will float chopped scallions on top. Serve at once with the crackers.

BAKED WINTER SQUASH SOUP

I DON'T REMEMBER winter squash growing up, but now they are one of the first signs of the change of seasons. They come in all colors inside and out. My personal favorites are butternut and Hubbard. These days you may also find interesting Asian varieties at the market. Sometimes these squash are so brightly colored that the resulting soup looks like bowls of paint going out to the table. I love this kind of garishness. You ought to see my house.

Serves 8–10

3–3½ pounds winter squash

1 teaspoon salt

½ teaspoon freshly ground black pepper

1 tablespoon strong chili powder

2 teaspoons whole cumin seeds

10 cloves garlic, peeled

2 tablespoons (packed) light brown sugar

2 tablespoons (¼ stick) unsalted butter

⅛ teaspoon dried red pepper flakes

3–4 cups heavy cream

½ cup roasted, salted pumpkin seeds, for garnish

Preheat oven to 400°F. Wash the squash and split it lengthwise. Scoop out the seeds and dust the cut side of each with salt and pepper. Arrange in a baking pan cut side up. Divide the chili powder, pepper flakes, cumin seeds, and garlic evenly among the squash cavities. Top each cavity with the brown sugar and then the butter, again divided evenly. You may make two layers of squash if you need to. Cover the pan either with its lid or with foil. If you use foil, put a piece of kitchen parchment over the squash first to keep it from reacting with the aluminum.

Bake until very soft, 60–90 minutes depending on the type and size of the squash. The garlic should easily mash with a fork.

When they are done and have cooled enough to be handled, scoop out the flesh, the garlic, and any juice that may be in the hollow of the squash. Use a food mill or food processor to puree. Taste the juice in the bottom of the roasting pan. If it is bitter, throw it out. If it is delicious, save it to add to the soup. Transfer the puree to a soup pot and thin with enough heavy cream to make it souplike—probably 3 cups, but this will vary because different squash will have different moisture content. Simmer for 15 minutes to bond the flavors. Do not boil. Taste and correct the seasoning. Serve hot with the pumpkin seeds on top. You can substitute half-and-half for the heavy cream if you would like to serve the soup cold, but omit the simmering.

BAKED SWEET POTATO SOUP

I LOVE TO USE white sweet potatoes in this recipe, but any variety will do. This soup is equally good hot or cold.

Serves 4–6

3 pounds sweet potatoes

2 cups freshly squeezed orange juice

3 tablespoons peeled, grated fresh ginger

½ teaspoon dried red pepper flakes

1½–2 cups heavy cream

2 teaspoons salt

Dash of Tabasco or other hot pepper sauce

half-and-half or whole milk (optional)

Freshly grated nutmeg, for garnish

Preheat the oven to 350° F. Wash the sweet potatoes, pierce them in several places with the tip of a sharp knife, and bake them in their skins until very soft, approximately 1 hour. They cook more evenly if you turn them over once. When they are completely done and cool enough to handle, peel them and puree in a food mill. If you have patience but no food mill, mash them with a potato masher and then press them through a sieve with the back of a spoon to remove any lumps. Stir the orange juice into the puree. Add the ginger and pepper flakes. Add enough of the heavy cream to produce the consistency of soup and simmer over low heat for 20 minutes. Do not boil or the soup may break. Correct the seasoning with salt and a dash of Tabasco. You may want to strain the soup through a sieve if the ginger fibers are too noticeable.

If you decide to serve this cold, you will need to thin it further with either milk or half-and-half. In either case, serve with a grating of fresh nutmeg on top.

DUCK AND ONION SOUP

To make this soup, you must first have a delicious rich stock. My personal favorite is a stock made from the browned bones of ducks I dress for other recipes.

Serves 4–6

1 tablespoon unsalted butter

3 large onions, peeled, halved, and thinly sliced

¼ cup bourbon or brandy

10 cups Duck Stock (page 16)

2 teaspoons salt

1 teaspoon freshly ground black pepper

1 teaspoon (packed) light brown sugar (optional)

1 tablespoon Worcestershire sauce

French bread, cut into 1-inch slices and toasted

¾ cup grated Swiss cheese

¼ cup Salt-Cured Duck Legs (page 47) (optional)

Place the butter and the onions in a dutch oven with a tight-fitting lid. Cover and simmer on the lowest possible heat for at least 30 minutes but longer if you have time. Sometimes I put this on first thing in the morning and don't finish the soup until afternoon.

The onions will produce a great deal of liquid. Uncover and allow the liquid to reduce on a little higher heat. You want the onions to be soft but to not have colored at all. When the liquid is nearly gone, about 15 minutes, and you have no other distractions, turn the heat up full tilt. The onions will begin a hard boil. Stir constantly. When the liquid is all but gone and the onions are looking thick and glossy, switch from a spoon to a metal spatula. The onion sugars will have begun to caramelize in the bottom of the pot. Scrape this off and stir it back into the onions. Continue scraping and clearing the bottom for as long as you can. At some point you will begin to fall behind and the onions will be in danger of burning. The onions should be dark reddish brown but not burned at all. Pick out any black bits. Pull the pot away from the heat, add the whiskey, and stand back. Nudge the pot back over the fire. It will ignite suddenly with a whoosh. This is dramatic but not dangerous. Stir down the fire with a long-handled wooden spoon. Add the stock, reduce the heat to medium-high, and allow the soup to cook at a low boil for at least 1 hour, longer if you can.

Taste the soup. If it is not very rich, turn up the heat and reduce it more. Season with salt and black pepper. The caramelized onions should have imparted a faint sweetness, but if they have not, you may cheat by adding the brown sugar. Add the Worcestershire sauce to finish off the seasoning.

To serve, put a slice of the French bread and 2 tablespoons of shredded Swiss cheese in the bottom of each bowl and then fill with hot soup.

To make this into a main course, shred some of your Salt-Cured Duck Legs (page 47) into the soup right before serving, just long enough to heat it through.

MASHED RUTABAGAS

RUTABAGAS ARE THE cheapest of all vegetables, including cabbage. When I was little, I hated rutabagas. We only had them at my aunt Hi's house. She loved them and grew them in her garden. They are a good winter crop here in North Carolina. Years later, a roommate with a New England background made them for me like mashed potatoes, and I've been devoted ever since. We have people who call the restaurant in the fall to see when they will be back on the menu. We serve them with lots of main courses and also as a side dish.

Serves 4–6

2½ pounds rutabagas

Water

2 teaspoons salt

6 tablespoons unsalted butter

3 cloves garlic, peeled and minced

½ teaspoon freshly ground black pepper

Peel and dice the rutabagas. Be careful: when raw, they are very hard and may roll suddenly when you apply the knife with enough force to cut them. Place them in a roomy pot with enough water to cover them. Add a teaspoon of the salt and bring to a boil. They will take a lot longer to cook than potatoes, 25–30 minutes. When done, they should pierce easily with a fork. Drain in a colander and allow them to dry for a while from their own heat. Then mash as you would potatoes.

Melt the butter in a saucepan with the garlic. Let it bubble for a second but don't let the garlic brown. Fold into the rutabagas along with the pepper and more salt, if needed.

If there are any leftovers, they will reheat well.

BRUSSELS SPROUTS

THIS IS ANOTHER food that I didn't much like growing up. I think it is because people tended to overcook them. I prefer to steam them, and that's about the whole recipe.

Serves 4–6

1½ pounds brussels sprouts

2 tablespoons (¼ stick) unsalted butter

1 teaspoon salt

Trim off the stems of the brussels sprouts with a sharp paring knife and make a little **X** in the bottom of each sprout. Cook in a steamer at full boil for about 8 minutes. These go really fast. The sprouts should still be firm, pretty, and green (not olive colored), but the knife blade should go to the center easily. Quickly drop them into ice water to stop the cooking. All this can be done in advance, as the brussels sprouts can be quickly reheated at serving time in the steamer or in simmering water. This cook likes to roll them in butter and salt and eat them like popcorn while he works. Serve hot.

SCALLOPED POTATOES

PEOPLE ALWAYS ASK for this recipe. Because the gratin is so rich and thick, they want to know what kind of cheese is in it. There is none.

To prepare these potatoes, you will need a shallow, 2-quart baking dish that can be used both on top of the stove and in the oven. A 12-inch cast-iron skillet would do. I use an old French cast-iron gratin at home.

Serves 10–12

2 tablespoons (¼ stick) unsalted butter, melted

6 cloves garlic, peeled and chopped

1 teaspoon dried marjoram

¼ teaspoon dried red pepper flakes

4 large baking potatoes, peeled and thinly sliced

1½ teaspoons salt

½ teaspoon freshly ground black pepper

1½ cups half-and-half

1½ cups heavy cream

Preheat the oven to 350° F. Place the butter in a large pan on top of the stove over high heat and swirl it around to coat the bottom. As the butter begins to sizzle, add the garlic, marjoram, and pepper flakes. As soon as this begins to smell wonderful remove it from the heat. You don't want browned garlic or burned herbs. Fill the pan with layers of sliced potatoes. Broadcast the salt and pepper over the top and wash this down with the half-and-half. Return the pan to the stovetop and turn the heat on full blast. When the butter begins to bubble up through the half-and-half, drizzle the heavy cream all over the top of the potatoes.

Place the gratin in the oven, uncovered, for 60 to 70 minutes. Baste from time to time. The potatoes are done when they are completely tender and the top has become pretty and brown. Let the potatoes rest for 10 minutes before serving. This is a great side dish for steaks or for roast chicken.

There are endless variations of this recipe. Sliced mushrooms and onions are a good addition. Lately, I've been doing a winter version with sweet potatoes, celery root, parsnips, and carrots. No white potatoes at all. In the summer, odds and ends from the garden can be used: some sliced tomatoes, fresh herbs, sliced squash, even beets (although the color will be startling). And hot chiles are *very good* baked in heavy cream.

USING A WHOLE DUCK

DUCKS ARE VERY MUCH like pigs in that you can make use of every speck. Once upon a time ducks were roasted and served whole. I almost never roast a duck whole anymore. I dismantle it and produce four or five different dishes with its parts.

Boning a duck is both logical and simple. You will need a sharp boning knife. Duck skin seems to dull a knife more quickly than much tougher foods, so have a sharpening steel at hand. Run your finger down the middle of the breast, feeling the center ridge of the breastbone. If you press hard enough the outline of the bone will be visible. Slice the breast along this center ridge from the cavity to the wishbone (in other words, from one end to the other). Then, using the knife blade, carefully peel away the meat from each half of the breast from the bones. Start at the cavity and work back toward the legs and wings. Try to leave as little meat as possible on the skeleton. Ducks are conveniently divided up by ridges of fat, so you will come to a thin boundary of it as you finish removing the breast meat from the carcass. Sever the meat along this line of fat.

When the breast meat is removed, pop the leg bones out of their joints and cut the legs and thighs away in one piece. There are lines of fat to guide you here as well. Again, leave as little meat as possible on the carcass. Go as slowly as you need to. The only tricky part is around the wishbone, and this is easy to figure out once you see it.

From each duck you will have two breast portions (ideal for Seared Duck Breast, page 49) and two leg and thigh combos (for Salt-Cured Duck Legs, page 47). If you wish to use them, there are also two meaty wings. My Vietnamese friends roast these with salt until they are dark brown and crunchy. Lastly, there are lots of skin trimmings that can be rendered into cracklings, a carcass and giblets that can be browned and turned into soup or sauce (or not browned and turned into Chinese soup), and livers for Two- (or Three-) Bird Pâté (page 27).

SALT-CURED DUCK LEGS

I have used these legs in both jambalaya and in baked beans. The meat can also be shredded into soup or tossed with a hot vinaigrette and some walnuts to dress a wilted salad. This winter in Quebec, I was served a single leg, warmed through and crisped up in a broiler on a lettuce leaf as a first course. Usually I only preserve the legs this way, but once for Christmas I cured whole ducks for presents and it worked beautifully.

Serves 6–8

1 small knob of fresh ginger, peeled and thinly sliced

5 cloves garlic, peeled

1 tablespoon freshly grated nutmeg

10 whole cloves

10 whole allspice berries

10 whole juniper berries

5 pieces star anise

1 cup salt

Pinch of dried red pepper flakes

6–8 duck legs, well rinsed and patted dry

10 teaspoons fennel seeds

6–8 cups lard or rendered duck fat, or a combination of the two

Put the ginger and garlic in the bowl of a food processor and puree. Add the nutmeg, cloves, allspice, and any other hard spices you have chosen. Grind for a minute to break this up. Then feed in the salt and pepper flakes. If the ginger or garlic are especially juicy, you can add more salt. You want the mixture to be granular rather than a paste.

Rub the legs all over with the salt mixture. A thin coating is sufficient. You will have salt left over. Pack the duck in a glass or stainless steel container and let cure for at least 10 days, covered in the refrigerator. A week longer is okay. The longer they sit, the saltier they become. Inspect them from time to time and pour off the juice they will produce, adding a little more of the salt to replace what has melted away.

Rinse the duck legs and then submerge them in cool water. Let them soak refrigerated overnight.

Heat the oven to 250° F. Rinse and pat dry the duck legs. Layer them in a dutch oven or tall-sided roasting pan with a top (and a rack, if possible). In France they are cooked submerged in goose or duck fat, but I never have enough of that so I use lard.

Melt enough lard to completely submerge all of the legs. Cover the legs with the fat, cover the pot, and place the duck in the oven. At such a low temperature, this takes a very long time. Begin testing them for doneness after 4 hours. I don't remember where I first heard this next instruction, but it is my favorite one in cooking and it is also absolutely true: the ducks should cook until they are tender enough that a broom straw may be passed through the thickest part without bending or breaking.

Let the duck cool in the fat. It will keep for weeks in the congealed grease in the refrigerator and in fact is improved by sitting for a few days before using. I reuse the grease over and over during the duck season and with each use it takes on more and more of the duck flavor. Beneath the grease you will find a thin layer of tasty but very salty gelatin (called *salarc*) that I sometimes cut into tiny cubes to decorate pâtés or cold meats.

SEARED DUCK BREAST WITH AIGRE-DOUX

Serves 6

6 boneless duck breasts (see page 46), well rinsed and patted dry

1 teaspoon salt

3 cups Basic Sauce for Duck (page 50)

Preheat the oven to 400° F. Score the skin on top of each duck breast with a sharp knife. Cut all the way through the fat, but try not to cut into the meat beneath. Four or five cuts will do. Salt the meat on both sides.

Heat a dry skillet on top of the stove until a drop of water sizzles away instantly. Put the duck breasts, skin side down in the skillet. It should hiss and stick in place. This will be smoky. After 4 or 5 minutes you will be able to lift the duck breast. The skin should be pretty and brown and there should be rendered fat in the skillet. Brown the duck breasts on the other side now, about 2 minutes. Pour off the fat and put the skillet of duck into the oven (skin side back up). I like duck breast hot all the way through but still a little rare. This can take up to 5 minutes, depending on the size. For medium-rare, cook for 7 minutes, 9 minutes for medium. As a rule the firmer the meat is to the touch, the more well done it is. Remove from the oven and let it rest for 5 minutes. Slice thinly and arrange on plates. Catch all the juice from carving and add to the sauce. Spoon sauce over the duck.

BASIC SAUCE FOR DUCK

There are many variations of this recipe. The sauce is actually delicious plain, but I have suggested several fruits that may be added to fancy it up. I spoon the sauce over the duck breasts at the very last second so that the skin will remain crispy.

Makes About 4 cups

½ cup sugar

¼ cup red wine vinegar

1 quart Duck Stock (page 16)

½ cup heavy cream

1 cup of fruit (such as grapefruit sections, thinly sliced lemon rounds, cranberries, split seeded kumquats, or pitted sour cherries)

1 cup white wine

1 tablespoon unsalted butter

Put ¼ cup of the sugar and the vinegar in a heavy-bottomed saucepan. Stir a little to begin to dissolve the sugar and bring to a boil. When the mixture begins to look thick, but before it begins to brown around the edges, add the Duck Stock. Reduce to 1½ cups (25–30 minutes) and add the cream. Reduce again until the sauce begins to thicken a little. All this can be done in advance.

Combine the white wine with the remaining ¼ cup of the sugar. Use half this mixture to briefly blanche the cranberries or cherries. (The citrus fruits can be used as-is.) Drain them before adding to the sauce. The other half is to be refrigerated and retained to refresh the fruit and set the color. This can be done in advance as well.

At serving time, reduce the sauce again in a small saucepan until thick and lustrous-looking. Add the fruit of choice and swirl the pan. In all likelihood the fruits' liquid will dilute the sauce a little, so reduce it back down. Grapefruit sections will fall apart if they are cooked for long, so I quickly warm them in the sauce and remove them to the duck breasts at once before I finish reducing the sauce. Lastly, swirl in a little of the whole butter. Keep moving the pan until the butter is completely absorbed and spoon over the duck. Serve immediately.

FRIED GREEN TOMATOES WITH SWEET CORN AND LEMON BEURRE BLANC

This recipe works well with any green tomatoes, either those you are forced to pick on the night of the first frost or with those awful things you find in the grocery store in winter that are supposed to be ripe. Make the sauce first; then fry the tomatoes.

Serves 4–6

¾ cup all-purpose flour

2 teaspoons salt

1 teaspoon freshly ground black pepper

2 large eggs

3 tablespoons milk

¾ cup bread crumbs

5 large green tomatoes (about 8 ounces each),
   cut into half-inch slices

6 (¾ stick) tablespoons unsalted clarified butter

Corn and Lemon Beurre Blanc (page 53)

You will need three small bowls. In one put the flour seasoned with salt and pepper. In a second bowl, beat together the eggs and milk. Place the bread crumbs in a third bowl. Dredge the tomatoes first in the flour, then in the egg wash, and finally in the bread crumbs. Fry them in clarified butter, on medium-high heat, until hot through and pretty and brown, about 1½ minutes per side. Top with the sauce.

CORN AND LEMON BEURRE BLANC

3 cups (4–6 servings)

2 cups water

½ teaspoon salt

Kernels from 3 ears fresh corn, or 1½ cups frozen corn

2 large shallots, peeled and diced (about ½ cup)

Zest of 1 lemon

Juice of 3 lemons (about ½ cup)

1 cup dry white wine

1 bay leaf

½ teaspoon whole peppercorns

2 tablespoons heavy cream

12 tablespoons (1½ sticks) unsalted butter, cold and diced

Bring the water and salt to a boil. Blanch the corn for 4 minutes. Drain and keep warm.

Put the shallots, lemon zest, lemon juice, wine, and seasonings, in a small nonreactive saucepan. Bring to a boil and reduce until almost dry, about 4 minutes, but be careful not to let the shallots brown at all. Add the cream and bring back to a boil. When the reduction begins to thicken, turn off the heat, and begin to whisk in the butter bit by bit. Completely incorporate each bit before adding the next. By the time all the butter has been added, the sauce will be thick and lustrous. Strain the sauce through a fine sieve and stir in the corn. Hold in a warm sauceboat while you fry the tomatoes. If the sauce becomes too cool, it can be rewarmed *carefully* over very low heat if you stir constantly.

PORK ROAST WITH SAUERKRAUT

WE ALWAYS HAVE a pork roast with sauerkraut at holiday meals, a holdover from "those mean Yankee Germans" no doubt. My Aunt Mary Catherine usually brings it. I developed this recipe for the restaurant because we accumulate so many roasts in the freezer from dressing whole pork loins.

Serves 6 generously

1 pork roast (perhaps a 3–4 pound Boston butt)

2 teaspoons salt

1 teaspoon freshly ground black pepper

2 tablespoons bacon grease or cooking oil

2 pounds sauerkraut (bagged, not canned), rinsed

3 large carrots, peeled and sliced thickly

3 large parsnips, peeled and sliced thickly

1 sprig fresh rosemary

2 cups Chicken Stock (page 15)

Preheat the oven to 350° F. Rinse and pat dry the roast. Salt and pepper the roast and brown it on all sides in the bacon grease in a dutch oven with a tight-fitting lid. After the roast is browned, pour off the oil and tuck in half of the rinsed sauerkraut all around the roast halfway up the dutch oven. Add the vegetables and rosemary and cover with the rest of the sauerkraut. Add the stock. Cover tightly and bake for 2¼ hours until the meat is tender and easy to pull from the bones. Serve with mashed potatoes.

CASHEW CAKE WITH MADAME CONSTANCE'S MAPLE FROSTING

IF YOU ARE ever invited to my house for dinner, some form of this cake will likely be your dessert. I rarely have time to entertain at home, so I like to make something familiar and quick. This recipe calls for cashews, but I have used pecans, almonds, pistachios, and hazelnuts. I have iced it with lemon curd, whipped cream, and in this instance a sort of buttercream made from maple syrup, a recipe I learned years ago in Quebec from a wonderful cook.

Madame Constance was the housemother of a remote youth hostel on the northeastern shore of the St. Lawrence River at Sault-au-Mouton. She had another maple sugar trick that I have never quite been able to duplicate. She served hot blueberry cobbler. On top she first put vanilla ice cream. Then she poured ice cold heavy cream. *Then* she immediately poured boiling hot maple sugar over the whole thing, creating a sort of web of taffy all over the cobbler. I've never forgotten it.

Serves 8–10

2 tablespoons (¼ stick) unsalted butter, softened to room temperature

1½ pounds raw cashews

3 cups sugar

zest of 1 large orange

2 teaspoons cider vinegar

1 teaspoon salt

2 cups egg whites (about 16 eggs, with yolks reserved for frosting)

¼ teaspoon cream of tartar

¾ cup sifted all-purpose flour

Madame Constance's Maple Frosting (page 56)

Preheat oven to 350° F. Butter two 9-inch springform pans, line them with parchment, and butter and flour the parchment.

Grind the cashews coarsely with half of the sugar and the orange zest in a food processor. Cashews are very oily, so beware that they are not ground so far as to begin to form a paste. Toss with a bit of flour to help keep the nut meal separate.

Rinse a mixing bowl with the vinegar. Swirl in the salt. Shake the bowl over the sink, but don't wipe it out. In it, beat the egg whites with the cream of tartar and then the rest of the sugar. Beat until soft peaks form. Fold the egg whites into the nuts by thirds, and with the last third gently include the sifted flour. Divide the batter between the two cake pans.

Bake for about 1 hour. The cake should be pretty and brown and a toothpick or broom straw should come out clean when inserted at the center. Allow to cool on racks for at least 1 hour before removing the springforms.

Each cake will be a layer. The cakes must be absolutely cool before they can be iced or the icing will spoil.

MADAME CONSTANCE'S MAPLE FROSTING

This will be a cinch if you have ever made buttercream icing. You will need an electric mixer.

2 cups of frosting, enough for a two-layer cake

8 large egg yolks

¾ cup sugar

½ cup Grade B pure maple syrup

1 pound unsalted butter, cut into small bits and softened

Beat the egg yolks with the whisk attachment of an electric mixer for 10 minutes or so on high until they have become pale yellow. Combine the sugar and the maple syrup in a saucepan and bring them to a boil that can't be stirred down, about 3 minutes.

Reduce the mixer speed to medium and slowly drizzle the maple syrup in a thin stream into the egg yolks. Aim so that you don't hit the whisk and sling the hot sugar out into the room. Add all the syrup. Turn off the mixer and scrape down the bowl with a spatula. Return the mixer to high speed. The egg yolks will be fairly hot, so beat the mixture until it has cooled back down to room temperature. Don't cheat. The eggs must be cool enough so that the butter does not melt when added to them. When the side of the mixing bowl feels cool, add the butter, bit by bit until it is all absorbed.

This recipe will make enough frosting to put between the layers and to ice the outside of the two cashew layers. Needless to say, this is very sweet, so sometimes I put barely sweetened whipped cream between the layers and on top of the cake and only use the frosting on the sides. The extra frosting will re-frigerate fairly well for a week if tightly wrapped in plastic. It must be softened very slowly at room temperature and applied with a warm knife or spatula.

PERSIMMON PUDDING
FROM CROOK'S CORNER

MY EDITOR SUGGESTED that I include at least one recipe from Crook's Corner that was not my own. I chose this pudding, which is my very favorite recipe from my inherited repertoire. Most people would expect me to choose shrimp and grits because it has become so famous, but I think that this is one of the best recipes from Bill's books. I was glad to do this because it gives me an opportunity to talk about something that comes up all the time: Do I have a problem following in the footsteps of such a famous chef? Chefs' egos are legendary, and many people suppose that I might resent the shadow. No, I don't. This could be a problem for someone who is unpleasantly ambitious, but I've always seen it as an advantage. What if I had to come up with something else to replace all these wonderful recipes every day? I can barely finish all my work as it is.

When I first came to Crook's Corner, I would have been quite lost without the four little clear plastic boxes of recipe cards that still sit on a shelf by the back door. They contain the backbone of this restaurant's reputation, and I would never dream of altering a one of them. The slaw, the hush puppies, and indeed the shrimp and grits need no improvement.

For years I've been getting wild persimmons from my friend Mary Andrews. They grow around one of her pastures. I have to compete with the deer for them, but usually there are enough for us all. Get these if you can. They grow all over the eastern part of the United States. Remember that these are weeds, not gourmet items, and they needn't cost a fortune. Cultivars in the grocery store often cost a dollar apiece, thus rendering the pudding unaffordable.

Bear in mind that between its original version and this page this recipe has been quadrupled, adapted to mass production, translated into Spanish and then back into English, and finally cut back down for home use.

Serves 8–10

3 cups persimmons

2 cups buttermilk

1 tablespoon plus 1 stick unsalted butter, at room temperature

1½ cups sugar

3 large eggs

1½ cups all-purpose flour

½ teaspoon salt

1 teaspoon baking powder

1 teaspoon baking soda

½ teaspoon freshly grated nutmeg

½ teaspoon ground ginger

1 teaspoon cinnamon

Preheat oven to 350° F. Grease a 4 × 8 × 12-inch baking pan with 1 tablespoon of butter. Puree the persimmons, which will reduce them from 3 cups to 2 cups. (I prefer to use an old-fashioned food mill such as a Mulinex, but they may be pressed through a sieve or cone strainer.) Combine the puree with the buttermilk. Beat the stick of butter and the sugar in the bowl of an electric mixer with the paddle attachment until fluffy. Add the eggs one by one. By hand, in a large mixing bowl, stir the persimmons into the butter.

Sift all the dry ingredients together and fold them into the persimmon mixture. Put the batter into the baking pan, and place the pan in a larger pan and fill halfway up with warm water. Bake, uncovered, for 1¼ hours, or until the pudding is firm at the center, has pulled away from the sides of its pan, and a paring knife inserted into the center of the pudding comes out clean.

Serve hot with fresh whipped cream. This keeps well in the refrigerator for 4 or 5 days and reheats beautifully in the oven or microwave.

POACHED PEARS

THIS IS A RECIPE in two variations. Lately, I've been using the white wine version, but I am equally fond of the red one. The procedure for both is nearly the same and both are served in a pool of Crème Anglaise (page 62). The white wine version has a second sauce of caramel.

Serves 6

Water to cover the pears

6 nearly ripe pears, with pretty shapes and no blemishes

1 fresh lemon

2 cups either red or white wine

2 cups water

2 cups sugar

1 split vanilla bean

½ teaspoon whole peppercorns

¼ teaspoon whole cloves (for red wine recipe only; omit for white wine recipe)

¼ teaspoon whole allspice (for red wine recipe only; omit for white wine recipe)

6 pretty bay leaves

Crème Anglaise (page 62)

Caramel Sauce (for white wine recipe only; page 62)

Put enough water in a large bowl to cover all of the pears. Zest the lemon and reserve the zest. Squeeze the lemon into the bowl of water. Carefully peel each pear, trying to maintain its shape. Use a melon baller to remove the seeds from each pear, going in from the bottom of the fruit through the blossom. Put the pears in the lemon water as you finish them to prevent discoloring.

Stir the wine, water, and sugar together in a nonreactive saucepan. Add the lemon zest, vanilla bean, peppercorns, cloves (red wine recipe only), and allspice (red wine recipe only), and bring to a boil. Simmer on medium heat for 10 minutes. Poach the pears, a few at a time, as space will allow, in the simmering liquid. Don't let it boil hard. Cooking time will vary because different pears have different densities, but start checking after 10 minutes. A boning knife should pass all the way through the fattest part of the flesh without resistance. It is important to cook the pears thoroughly because any raw parts will discolor. Remove the pears from their poach as they are done, reserving the vanilla bean for the Crème Anglaise. When all are cooked, put them in a dish or bowl and pour the cooking liquid over them. They may be stored in this liquid. Chill the pears.

To serve, put 2 or 3 tablespoons of Crème Anglaise on a dessert plate. Place a pear in the middle. It's okay if some of the syrup or spices cling to them. Insert a bay leaf in each pear next to the stem. If you have made the recipe with white wine, drizzle 2 tablespoons of caramel sauce over the pear. Serve either recipe with cookies.

These sauces are difficult to make in small amounts, but it is hard to imagine not being able to find a use for any leftovers.

CRÈME ANGLAISE

Makes about 2 cups (enough for 6 pears)

6 large egg yolks

½ cup sugar

1½ cups milk

Reserved vanilla bean from the pear poach

Beat the egg yolks and sugar together in a small bowl. Scald the milk with the vanilla bean in a medium saucepan. Don't boil it, just let it begin to steam. Slowly beat the milk into the egg yolks in a thin, steady stream. Return everything to the saucepan and cook carefully over low heat, stirring constantly until the custard has thickened slightly. Sometimes this happens quickly, sometimes not. The custard should coat the back of the spoon when ready. Strain the Crème Anglaise into a sauceboat and chill. Discard the vanilla bean. This sauce will keep for a week in the refrigerator.

CARAMEL SAUCE

Makes about 3 cups (more than enough for 6 pears, but it's hard to make any less)

2 cups sugar

4 tablespoons water

1 cup heavy cream

½ teaspoon vanilla extract

Mix the sugar and water together in your heaviest frying pan. Place the pan over high heat. Shake the pan and stir the sugar continuously with a long-handled wooden spoon. The sugar will first melt and then begin to color within 5 or 6 minutes. Keep moving the browning sugar. The hotter and more caramelized it becomes, the more liquid it will become as well. The sugar will continue to darken. When it is about the color of peanut butter, turn off the heat and dump in the cream all at once. Be careful. It will boil up suddenly and give off a lot of steam. Try to stand back and stir rapidly at the same time. While the boiling subsides, continue stirring. Remember that caramel is very, very hot. Place the pan somewhere, safe and out of the way to cool, for about 15 minutes when safe to touch again. Stir in the vanilla extract. Store in a Pyrex measuring cup. This sauce is best used hot. If you are not using it right away, it can be warmed up successfully in the microwave. Extra sauce will keep for two weeks refrigerated.

WINTER

I OFTEN THINK THAT MY LIFE could be documented by a series of great dinner parties. Some, especially from childhood, are just memory fragments, while others are quite distinct. In the winter of 1973 I found myself traveling with friends across Canada, from Halifax to Victoria. The politics of war colored everything in those days, and on this trip we constantly crossed paths with the American exile community. In winter we tend to move toward hearth and home, but those were singularly uncozy days and I remember often feeling unsettled, as if I were an outlaw.

It was the policy of Pierre Trudeau's government to promote more friendly feelings between the English- and French-speaking communities in Canada. That country had been, in reality, two separate ones within a loose national framework. Part of Trudeau's policy was the creation of a system of youth hostels all over the country. The hope was that the youth of both groups would travel and get a better feeling for the nation as a whole.

On a snowy November night in such a hostel at Edmonton, in Alberta, it fell to me somehow to produce dinner for the large crowd of boarders.

Some hostels were presided over by a kind of housemother. Others were more free form and that was the case in Edmonton. Food for these places was often donated and would appear magically in the common kitchen. My menu that night was to include six or seven pig spines with tails still attached, a case of over-the-edge tomatoes with lots of spots and blemishes, some sprouted onions, and some frozen corn. There was a large iron stew pot. The result was a miraculous hearty soup. The hostel was full of all kinds of kids that night: English and French Canadians, American visitors, and two Native American boys for whom French was a second language and English was unknown. The stew was plenty for all, and soon the small groups of travelers had amalgamated into a warm, cordial dinner party. We took up a beer money collection and sat up late into the cold Alberta night telling stories, singing songs, smoking dope, and watching the fireplace. Outside, the aurora borealis was glorious. We slept in heaps under blankets on the living room floor that night, drifting off one by one, rather than returning to our bedrooms. In the morning we all went our separate ways.

Wintry nights lend themselves to cozy dinner parties. It doesn't snow a lot here, but when it does the effects can be pleasantly paralyzing. For years roommates and I kept the fixings for a cassoulet on hand all winter in hopes of being stranded.

SOUP DAKAR

THE IDEA FOR this soup came from all directions. For my job at a French restaurant, it was a way to incorporate some colonial flavors into the menu as chefs in France often like to do. For my job at a Southern restaurant, it let me reference chicken country captain in a new way. The pappadams this recipe calls for are readily available at most Asian markets.

Serves 4–6

1 whole chicken (about 3 pounds)

1 teaspoon salt

1 tablespoon all-purpose flour

1 tablespoon curry powder

4 stalks celery, chopped (about 1 cup)

1 small onion, chopped (about 1 cup)

½ cup heavy cream

4 ounces mango chutney

½ cup more heavy cream (for cold soup only; omit for hot soup)

⅛ teaspoon cayenne pepper (for cold soup only; omit for hot soup)

¼ teaspoon dried red pepper flakes (for hot soup only; omit for cold soup)

6 cups cooked white rice (for hot soup only; omit for cold soup)

Fresh fried pappadams

Place the chicken in a soup pot and cover with cold water by 2 inches. Add the salt and bring to a boil. Cook for 15 minutes and then remove from heat and cover. Let stand for 20 minutes. Remove the chicken from the broth.

When the chicken is cool enough to handle, pick the meat from the carcass. Put the skeleton and the skin back into the broth and bring to a hard boil for at least another 20 minutes. The resulting stock should taste like delicious chicken noodle soup. Strain the stock, degrease it, and return it to a boil. If you are going to serve the soup hot you will add the meat back into the soup later. If you are going to serve the soup cold, use the meat to make chicken salad.

While your stock is boiling, mix the flour and curry powder and lightly brown them over medium heat in a small frying pan. Whisk the curry into the boiling stock. Add the celery and onion, ½ cup of cream, and the chutney, and reduce the soup to a simmer and cook for 30 minutes, stirring often to prevent the flour from sinking to the bottom and burning. Do not let the soup come to a full boil or it may separate.

At this point you must decide two things. First, is the chutney too chunky for your taste? If it is, pass the soup through a food mill or push it through a sieve with the back of a spoon.

Second, will the soup be served cold or hot? If the soup is to be served cold, chill it for a final degreasing. Add another half cup of cream and the cayenne. Taste for salt.

If the soup is to be served hot, bring it to a low simmer and add the chicken meat and a pinch of pepper flakes. Cook for 10 minutes to warm the chicken. Taste for salt. At serving time, put ½ cup of cooked rice in the bottom of each bowl and then fill with the soup.

Either hot or cold, lay a fresh fried pappadam on top of each bowl.

CHICKEN POT PIE

PEOPLE LOVE THIS when cold weather comes. I serve the pies in one-and-one-quarter-cup ramekins that look like little baked bean pots. I suppose that you could make one large pie, but I have never tried. In any case it is important to simmer the filling until it is well thickened because the pastry will not puff properly if it is sitting atop liquid. Make the pastry well in advance. The glutens need to rest and it needs to be very well chilled before you roll it out. The filling is also better if made ahead. Like soups and stews, the flavor develops better with a little time and the natural gelatins will have time to kick in for better thickening.

The pastry is a variation on the quick puff pastry that Julia Child introduced in her *Julia Child & Company* series on PBS back in the 1970s. Up until that time making puff pastry was an arduous task that most people would not try at home. Her new technique made it so unbelievably easy that people were tempted to use it almost casually. The first time you do this is as astonishing as the first time you make mayonnaise.

Makes 6 1¼-cup pies

PASTRY

3¼ sticks unsalted butter

2 cups all-purpose flour

¼ teaspoon salt

½ cup cold water with an ice cube in it

Flour for rolling out the pastry

1 egg yolk

1 teaspoon grainy mustard

FILLING

1 (about 3 pounds) velvetized chicken (see page 15)

1 medium onion, peeled and diced (about 1½ cups)

2 tablespoons (¼ stick) unsalted clarified butter

2 cups sliced mushrooms

2 large carrots, peeled and sliced into thin rounds (about 2 cups)

2 large parsnips, peeled and sliced into thin rounds (about 2 cups)

4 tablespoons (½ stick) unsalted butter

¼ cup all-purpose flour

1 pint pearl onions, peeled and blanched according to package
    instructions

1 cup frozen small green peas

To make the pie pastry: Dice the butter into quarter-inch cubes and toss with a little of the flour to keep them from sticking back together. Place in a large mixing bowl and refrigerate to rechill for at least 20 minutes.

Add the flour and salt to the butter and begin to combine them with your fingers as you would for making biscuits. Do this for a few minutes until they are thoroughly mixed and the size of the butter chunks is reduced by half. You do not want the butter to completely disappear. Add the water all at once (fish out any ice that hasn't melted) and stir together with a spatula. Dump out on a floured table or countertop. It will look like a crumbly mess. Shape it into a rectangle of approximately 4 inches high by 6 inches long. Use a rolling pin to roll it out into an 8 × 12-inch rectangle. You will do more flattening than rolling this first time, but try to apply equal force in all directions. The pastry will not want to hold together at this point. Even though it will want to fall apart, return the rectangle back to its original dimensions by folding the long dimension back on itself by thirds as if you were folding a letter to put into an envelope. Turn the rectangle 45 degrees and roll it back out to an 8 × 12-inch rectangle. Fold again. Repeat this rolling and folding twice more. With each turn, the pastry will become more and more cohesive. Wrap in plastic wrap and refrigerate for at least 20 minutes.

When the pastry has rested and is good and cold, roll and fold it two more times, always returning to the same 4 × 6-inch rectangle. It should now look like nice pie dough. Allow to rest at least an hour more before using, but it will keep easily for a week in the refrigerator.

When you are ready to make pies, roll out your dough and cut it into circles that are a quarter to half an inch larger than your pie ramekins. Beat together the egg yolk and the mustard in a small bowl. Paint each top with the egg mixture and freeze the tops solid. They will be put frozen on top of the pies at the very last second before baking.

To make the pie filling: Prepare the chicken. When it is cool enough to touch, pick the meat and reserve for the filling. Add the skin and bones back into the broth and cook it until you have about 1½ quarts of stock. Strain and degrease.

In a soup pot, sauté the onion in the clarified butter. When it is translucent, add the mushrooms and cook until all the butter is absorbed. Add the strained, degreased stock and bring to a simmer. Add the carrots and parsnips.

Put the butter in a saucepan and begin to soften it over medium heat. Whisk in the flour and turn up the heat. Stir constantly until the flour is a pale tan color, 8–10 minutes. Whisk this roux into the stock followed by the cream.

Simmer on medium heat, uncovered, for 45 minutes, or until the filling has begun to thicken considerably. You will need to stir this often to prevent scorching on the bottom. When it seems appropriately thick, add the chicken meat and the pearl onions. Bring back to a simmer and cook for 10 minutes more. The peas should be added right before the pies are put into the oven to bake so they won't turn olive-drab.

The filling can be used right away or cooled and used later. If used later, the filling should be reheated on the stove top or in a microwave before the pies are baked.

Preheat the oven to 375° F. Fill the ramekins with the filling. If it appears too runny, use a slotted spoon. Center the frozen tops on each pie. Bake at once for about 20 minutes. The filling will already be hot. The tops should be puffy and golden brown.

Serve with a green salad or a side of wilted spinach.

GREEN TABASCO CHICKEN

MY FRIEND SARA HUTT was living at my house the summer she studied for the bar. We had a small backyard garden and one of our most successful crops was hot chiles. We put up many bottles in vinegar. These vinegars became extremely hot. Mine sat in the refrigerator for months. By then Sara was living in Washington. In a phone conversation she mentioned that she had been marinating whole chickens in the vinegar before roasting them and that the results were delicious and surprisingly mild. Several years later the Tabasco company introduced a new product: Tabasco Jalapeño Sauce. This stuff is so delicious that I could drink it. I remembered Sara's recipe and adapted it thusly.

Serves 4–6

1 whole chicken (about 3 pounds), well rinsed and patted dry

1 teaspoon salt

½ teaspoon freshly ground black pepper

1 lemon

1 jalapeño

1 clove garlic, peeled

1 bottle Green Tabasco Jalapeño Sauce or other
   green hot pepper sauce
Melted butter or bacon grease, for basting
1½ cups of dry white wine

Preheat the oven to 500° F. Snip off the pope's nose (see Note) and the last joint of each of the chicken's wings. Salt and pepper the cavity and stuff it with the lemon, jalapeño, and garlic. Truss up the chicken with kitchen twine and place it on a rack in a roasting pan. Baste the chicken with a half a bottle of the Tabasco. Sprinkle salt and lots of black pepper on the wet Tabasco. Place the chicken in the oven.

Put the trimmings plus the giblets of the chicken, minus the liver, in a 1-quart saucepan and cover with cold water. Bring to a simmer and let it cook while the chicken roasts. This will be the base for the sauce.

In about 20 minutes you should begin to hear the chicken sizzling. When you do, reduce the heat to 350° F and baste the chicken with the butter or bacon grease. Repeat every 20 minutes. Cook until the legs can be wiggled easily. This should take between 1 and 1¼ hours. I prefer roasted chicken to be a little past done; it will be better cold the next day, if there is any left.

Let the chicken rest for 20 minutes on the counter. If it is then cool enough to handle, remove the string. Use poultry shears (if you cook chickens a lot, you really should buy these) to cut out the spine. Try to save all the juice that will be in the cavity. Put the juice, spine, jalapeño, and garlic into the sauce pot and turn up the heat to a heavy boil, but discard the lemon, as it will make the sauce bitter.

Place the roasting pan on top of the stove and turn the eye up high. Pour the wine onto it and use a metal spatula to scrape up all of the browned bits and drippings. Add all this to the sauce. Let it reduce until it begins to thicken. The time will vary according to the amount of liquid you begin with. Degrease.

Cut the chicken into serving pieces and arrange on a platter. When the sauce has reduced until it is thick and lustrous, strain it through a sieve over the chicken. If there is more sauce than the platter can hold, bring the rest to the table in a sauceboat.

We serve this with My Mashed Potatoes (page 122) and wilted spinach.

Note: The term *pope's nose* is used to refer to the tail of the chicken at one end of the spine. My very Catholic great-grandmother was fond of it (and bone marrow and pig knuckles, etc.). When she would use the term in polite company, my grandmother Annie and my aunt Theresa would roll their eyes heavenward and say, "Oh Mother, honestly!"

SCALLOPS WITH SPINACH AND HOMINY

ORIGINALLY, THIS RECIPE was for those nice little calico scallops that used to be plentiful off the North Carolina coast in winter. Now they seem to have been fished to near extinction, so we must use other small varieties. I think that this occurred to me originally because the scallops and the hominy are of similar size and shape. As it turns out, fried hominy complements scallops very well.

Mexican-style hominy was quite a revelation to me. I had grown up eating hominy browned in a skillet with breakfast, but I was never wild about it. Then one day someone on my staff made *posole* (chicken-and-hominy stew) for lunch. The hominy they used was crunchy, not mushy. I began at once using this improved version in soups, stews, and even salads. It can be found in any Latin American grocery store and they are everywhere.

Serves 4–6

1 cup superrefined sauce flour (such as Wondra or
    Shake & Blend)
1 teaspoon dried mustard
2 teaspoons salt
1 teaspoon freshly ground black pepper
2 pounds small bay scallops, patted dry
3 tablespoons clarified unsalted butter, for sautéing
2 cups of drained white Mexican-style hominy
6 cups spinach leaves, washed and left damp
Lemon wedges

Season the flour with the mustard, salt, and pepper. Taste this before you start to make sure that it is salty enough for you. Pat the scallops dry and toss them in the flour, then put them in a sieve and shake off the excess. Sauté over high heat in the clarified butter. Try not to crowd them as they will not cook evenly and the flour will make a paste with the butter. Let them brown ever so slightly on one side and then begin tossing them in the pan. Work quickly. Add the hominy and keep tossing the pan. Start adding the spinach. You may need to add it in batches as it cooks down. Think Chinese stir-fry. When the spinach is wilted but not cooked to death, the scallops are done. Serve with plenty of lemon wedges. This is a whole meal in one pan.

FISH BAKED IN PAPER

IN A BUSY RESTAURANT menu items like this make sense because all of the work is in the preparation. The service is almost instant, so it is also a good choice for a dinner party. I wrap the fish in kitchen parchment, which is a fairly common item these days. I'm explaining this particular presentation for the sake of instruction, but keep in mind that this technique is very versatile and you may use any ingredients you like. Your fish fillets should be as boneless as possible and they should be fairly thick. I have used fish both with and without skin. Some fish skin is tasty and some is very pretty.

Serves 6

RICE

1 small onion, peeled and finely diced (about ½ cup)

2 stalks celery, finely diced (about ½ cup)

2 tablespoons unsalted butter

2 cups long grain rice

1 teaspoon salt

2 cups heavy cream

3 cups Chicken Stock (page 15), vegetable stock, or seafood stock

1 cup freshly grated Parmesan cheese

1½ cups julienned carrots

6 teaspoons extra-virgin olive oil

4 ounces fresh baby spinach leaves, washed and left damp

6 fresh boneless mild fish fillets (6–7 ounces each), about 1 inch thick

2 teaspoons salt

1 teaspoon freshly ground black pepper

Zest of 1 lemon

6 small sprigs fresh herbs (such as thyme or tarragon)

Juice of 1 lemon

12 teaspoons dry vermouth

Preheat oven to 450°F. Place two baking sheets in the oven so they will be good and hot when it is time to cook the fish.

It is very important that the rice portion of the recipe be finished and cooled before you do anything else. You will essentially be making risotto that is not quite done.

Sauté the onion and celery in the butter in a steep-sided, heavy-bottomed pan. When the vegetables are translucent, add the rice and stir to coat it with butter. Begin adding the liquids in small amounts, alternating cream and stock, watching for the rice to approach doneness. Add the salt. You may or may not need all of the liquid. The rice should be thick and creamy, yet the grains should be firm and chewy. When the rice is all but done, stir in the cheese and spread the mixture out on a cool sheet pan to stop the cooking.

Bring a small saucepan of water to a boil. Blanch the carrots until just tender, about 30 seconds. Immediately transfer them to a bowl of ice water to set the color. Drain on a paper towel.

To assemble, you will need one 13 × 30-inch sheet of kitchen parchment per serving. Work with one sheet at a time. Paint one side of the sheet with the olive oil. Fold the sheet in half to mark the center; then unfold. When all the ingredients are in place, you are going to close one half over the other, like a book.

On one half of the paper, near the fold and in the center, place a 1-cup mound of the rice and press down into an inch-thick oval. Top with one-sixth of the spinach. Place a fish fillet on top of this. Tuck any stray spinach under the fish. Season with the salt and pepper. Top with a sixth of the lemon zest and a sixth of the carrots. Top with an herb sprig. Remember that how you arrange it now is how it will be seen by the diner. Sprinkle each piece of fish with a teaspoon of lemon juice and 2 teaspoons of vermouth.

Close the empty half of the paper over the fish as if you were closing a book. Starting at one end of the spine of this book, make small tight overlapping folds all the way around the paper. Take care to use enough paper in the fold so that no steam will be able to escape. The final result will resemble a large turnover made of paper.

Just before you want to eat, carefully arrange the packets on the hot sheet pans. It usually takes 10–12 minutes for these to cook. They are done when the paper is all puffy and full of steam. Remove each packet to a dinner plate and serve at once. A wonderful aroma will be released when they are opened at the table. The whole entrée is included in the paper. You need only a salad as an accompaniment.

CATFISH AMANDINE

EVERYBODY LIKES THIS except me. For some reason I've never warmed to catfish, but it is so popular that it appears often on my menu. Since catfish are widely farmed now (especially here in North Carolina), it is always available and I can get it when other seafood pickings are slim.

Serves 6

6 catfish fillets (8 ounces each)

1 cup buttermilk

½ cup Maseca instant corn masa mix

½ cup self-rising flour

1 teaspoon salt

½ teaspoon freshly ground black pepper

1 tablespoon sesame seeds

6 tablespoons (¾ stick) clarified butter

6 tablespoons (¾ stick) unsalted butter

1 cup sliced blanched almonds

Juice of 1 lemon (about ¼ cup)

Soak the catfish in the buttermilk for at least 30 minutes. Mix the Maseca, flour, salt, pepper, and sesame seeds together in a shallow pan. Shake off the fillets and dredge them in the flour mixture. Sauté in the clarified butter or oil until nicely browned on both sides, about 4 minutes per side. Catfish is very dense so you need to be sure that it is done through at its thickest part. Remove the fish to a warm platter and wipe out the sauté pan. Add the unsalted butter to the pan and turn up the heat to high. As soon as there is a little bit of melted butter, add the nuts. Swirl the pan constantly until the butter and the almonds are golden brown and smell nice and toasty. Quickly add the lemon juice to stop the cooking and immediately pour the sauce over the fish. Serve at once with a salad or Carrot Slaw (page 120).

Guts

Even when I was little, I liked liver. My mother and I would spar over the gizzards and hearts when we made fried chicken. Fried chicken livers at the K & W Cafeteria are my favorite lunch. I didn't encounter sweetbreads until I was grown up, but they are easy to love. If you can get people to try them before they know what they are, they will be hooked for life. And almost every year, for my birthday, I have veal brains with browned butter somewhere in Quebec.

Kidneys were more problematic. The first time I tasted them I thought I was going to choke. I can't imagine why I decided to try them again after that, but when I did a year later they had transformed miraculously into one of my favorite foods. I never pass them up on a menu now, except for when they are competing with veal brains with browned butter.

Chitlins I still can't do. I have tried. Fried are a little easier than boiled. I once got tricked by andouillette in France. After a bite or two I said to myself, "Hey, wait a minute, these are chitlins!" They actually were good, all stuffed and sausagey. I finished them, but I never ordered them again. I had begun this meal, by the way, with *museau,* a kind of head cheese made from the snout of a cow that always has fur in it. I can't resist ordering this to astound my dining companions.

Years ago on a visit to Bordeaux, the handwritten lunch menu on the blackboard seemed to advertise *coeurs en papillote.* "I think it says hearts in paper," I told my friend Mickey, "but it's hard to read." My French was less accomplished in those days, so my conversation with the waitress ended up with her striking her bosom with her fist repeatedly saying *"Coeur! Coeur!"* ever more loudly and distinctly. These were indeed hearts in paper—goose hearts. They were sliced in two, seasoned with salt, pepper, parsley, and thyme and splashed with vermouth. They were quickly baked in little envelopes of kitchen parchment and when they were torn open at the table the aroma was delightful. They are delicious. Today I save duck hearts in the freezer, and when I have collected enough, I can prepare them in this way for snacks for the class I give on how to use a whole duck.

So what is it about a plateful of entrails? Is it ancient Rome envy? A throwback to some kind of primitive savagery? Perhaps these cravings are best left unanalyzed. All I know is that when I'm sitting there with a big plate of kidneys, nobody else at the table picks at my dinner.

TWO RECIPES FOR VEAL SWEETBREADS

SWEETBREADS ARE NOT SWEET and have nothing to do with bread. Most other innards are called by name, but for some reason the thymus gland of the calf is named euphemistically. No deception is necessary. They are delicious. Just feed them to people before you tell them what they are and they are usually sold.

I'm including two different sauces for them, one plain and one fancy. The preparation of the sweetbreads themselves is always the same, whatever the sauce. I've never seen fresh sweetbreads. I'm told that they are too perishable. Purchase them a day before you plan to serve them so they can slowly thaw overnight in the refrigerator submerged in cool water.

Serves 4–6

1½ pounds sweetbreads

¼ cup white vinegar

3 cups dry white wine

4 teaspoons salt

1 tablespoon whole black peppercorns

1 tablespoon dried tarragon

1 bunch celery, with leaves, washed and coarsely chopped

Thaw the sweetbreads by submerging them in cool water overnight in the refrigerator. The next day, stir the vinegar into the thawing water and let them soak for 15 minutes. Put the wine, salt, peppercorns, tarragon, and celery into a pot with enough water to generously float the sweetbreads. Bring to a boil; then turn back to a simmer. Add the sweetbreads. Sweetbreads come in all sizes, so the cooking time will vary, but I have noticed that they usually float just as they are done. They should become firm to the touch at their thickest part but not so cooked that their surface has begun to flake off. Twenty minutes of simmering should be sufficient for most sweetbreads. When they are done, refresh them in a bath of ice water. Then drain them and weight them down in the refrigerator with a cast-iron skillet or some heavy canned goods for a few hours to firm them up further. When they are cold and solid, peel off the obvious membranes that cover them, and remove any large tubes or veins that you see. Some people like to slice them into rounds at this point, but I prefer to let them break into natural clumps as I clean them.

SWEETBREADS WITH BROWN BUTTER AND CAPERS

Serves 4–6

2 large eggs

1 teaspoon water

1½ pounds prepared sweetbreads (page 84)

2 cups stale bread crumbs

½ teaspoon salt

4 tablespoons (½ stick) clarified butter

4 tablespoons (½ stick) unsalted butter

Juice of 1 lemon (about ½ cup)

2 tablespoons capers, drained

1 tablespoon chopped fresh parsley

Beat the eggs with the water in a bowl that is big enough to hold the sweetbreads as well. Coat the sweetbreads with the eggs and then roll them in the bread crumbs that have been seasoned with the salt. Heat the clarified butter in a medium-sized skillet. Brown the sweetbreads on all sides and remove to a warm platter. Pour off the clarified butter, but try to retain some of the browned crumbs that will be in the skillet. Put the butter in the pan and turn the heat to high. Swirl the pan constantly until the butter becomes brown and smells toasty. Quickly add the lemon juice, followed by the capers and parsley. Pour the sizzling butter over the sweetbreads and serve at once.

SWEETBREADS WITH WILD TURKEY LIQUEUR

1 cup plain flour

½ teaspoon salt

¼ teaspoon freshly ground black pepper

1½ pounds prepared sweetbreads (page 84)

4 tablespoons (½ stick) clarified unsalted butter

1 cup thinly sliced mushrooms

¼ cup Wild Turkey Liqueur

¾ cup heavy cream

1 teaspoon freshly squeezed lemon juice

2 scallions (white and green parts), trimmed and chopped

Season the flour with the salt and pepper. Toss the sweetbreads in the flour to coat. Heat the clarified butter in a large sauté pan. Brown the sweetbreads on all sides, being careful not to crowd them. Remove them to a warm serving platter.

Add the mushrooms to the same pan and cook through. Pour off any butter that they do not absorb. Carefully pour in the Wild Turkey—it will flare up. Swirl the pan until the flames are gone. Add the cream and the lemon juice and bring to a boil. Return the sweetbreads to the sauce and simmer until it is thick and lustrous, 3 minutes at the most. Correct the seasoning. I often end up adding a few more drops of the liqueur and lemon juice at the last minute. Taste for salt and pepper. Stir in the scallions and serve at once.

OSSO BUCO

FROM TIME TO TIME, when I order bones for the stockpot, I open the box to discover perfectly sliced meaty veal shanks, that is, perfect osso buco. This is too un-Southern to serve at Crook's Corner, but I used to cook it a lot at La Residence. As a result, it is a favorite at staff reunions from those days. Most often now I cook it for staff lunch.

This recipe works best if you have a pot that is big enough to allow all the shanks to cook in a single layer. The dish can be either cooked in the oven for two to two and a half hours or simmered on the stovetop for a little less time.

Serves 6

1 cup all-purpose flour

3 teaspoons salt

2 teaspoons freshly ground black pepper

6 veal shanks (about 12 ounces each), about 1½ inches thick

6 tablespoons (¾ stick) clarified unsalted butter

3 cups dry white wine

Zest of 3 lemons

6–8 cups Chicken Stock (page 15)

3 bay leaves

6 tablespoons ketchup

1 pig's foot or a few veal knuckles (optional)

Preheat oven to 350° F if cooking the shanks in the oven.

Mix the flour with the salt and pepper in a shallow pan. Dredge the pieces of meat in the seasoned flour. Brown on both sides in the clarified butter. (I, of course, have discovered that the medallions of blood that ooze out of the marrow and fry up into little chips are delicious.) When you are through browning, pour off any excess butter, but try to keep as much as possible of the browned flour that has fallen in the pan. Return the pot to high heat and pour in the white wine. Let this boil down a bit until almost evaporated and add the lemon zest. Add enough stock to bring the level of the liquid even with the tops of the shanks. Finally, add 1 bay leaf and a capful of ketchup for each person. (I like to add a pig's foot or a couple of veal knuckles if I have them, to enrich the broth.) Cover tightly and cook in the oven for 2–2½ hours. If you prefer the stovetop method, simmer the shanks in a large dutch oven for about 2 hours. You want the meat to almost fall off the bone.

Serve this in large bowls with a big dollop of risotto (use the rice portion of the Fish Baked in Paper recipe, page 78), a side salad, and some fried bread (thin slices of french bread browned in olive oil) for the bone marrow.

CORNED HAM

THIS IS THE BEST ham in the world. They are common holiday fare in eastern North Carolina, taking their place alongside the turkey on holiday buffets, but they seem to be unknown almost everywhere else. My father used to send these hams to me several times a year by a Trailways bus. Finally, on a visit home, he took me to the Pak-A-Sak to meet the woman who made them for him so that I could learn to make my own. I've done so ever since. My teacher made them the old-fashioned way with salt rubbed into the ham. There is a newer version of the recipe where a salt solution is injected into the ham. Never buy one of these. They are tough and taste only of salt.

There is nothing quite like a corned ham. It's like a fresh pork roast, only really juicy and really salty. The color can be an unattractive gray, but otherwise a corned ham is perfection. I'm speculating here, but I think that these hams were probably the first ones eaten after slaughtering time each winter, making them by circumstance a short cure.

Serves a crowd

1 16–20-pound fresh ham
2 pounds kosher salt

Ask your butcher for a fresh ham. This is easier said than done these days since supermarkets mainly sell ready-to-eat varieties. It is much better if the ham is really fresh because ones that have been frozen, no matter how carefully they are thawed, seem to be tough. Rinse and dry the ham. There are three places where bones protrude: at each end and on one side near the hip end. Use a sharp knife to make incisions of about 3 inches deep along all three. Fill these incisions with salt (I use kosher salt but my teacher used plain Morton's table salt). Rub the outside of the ham all over with more salt. You want to cover the ham lightly, but you don't want a paste of salt. Place the ham in a nonreactive pan, cover with plastic wrap and then aluminum foil, and refrigerate. The Pak-A-Sak lady let her hams cure for 3 weeks. These are delicious but a little salty, so I have begun shortening the time to 11 days. All you have to do during the curing period is turn the ham from time to time, rerub it with salt, and pour off any juice that the ham has produced as it cures.

The day before you plan to cook the ham, wash it under cold running water. Be sure to flush out the salt pockets. Then submerge under clean cold water overnight.

Set the oven at 325° F. Put the ham on a rack in a covered roasting pan and bake for 20 minutes a pound. The internal temperature should reach 150° F for safety reasons, but I like to cook these hams until they start to fall off the bone. About 1½ hours before the ham is done, remove the cover and raise the oven to 375° F so the ham will brown. For the last 10 or so minutes I lift off the carapace of skin and set it beside the ham in the roasting pan. It will crisp up into the best cracklings ever.

People will stand around the platter picking long after dinner is done. More than once, when everyone has gone home, I've discovered a platter of bones.

At Crook's Corner we serve this ham with mashed potatoes with pan juices poured over both.

PORK CUTLETS WITH SLOW-COOKED ONIONS AND SIDE MEAT

I NEVER USE fewer than three pounds of onions for this because they cook down to almost nothing. Any leftovers will keep for a long time in the refrigerator. Outside of the South you may have to substitute pancetta for side meat.

Makes about 2 cups, enough for 6 servings

12 ounces side meat, skinned and cut into quarter-inch dice

1 tablespoon unsalted butter

3 pounds large onions, peeled, halved, and sliced thinly

2 teaspoons chopped fresh thyme

½ teaspoon freshly ground black pepper

6 prepared pork cutlets (see Cheese Pork with
   Madeira Sauce, page 92)

6 large eggs, fried sunny side up

Put the side meat and the butter in a heavy-bottomed pot with a tight-fitting lid. I use an old cast-iron dutch oven that Mexicans on my staff call *la abuela*— the grandmother. Cook on low heat until the butter has melted and the side meat has begun to release its grease. Be careful because side meat has a very low burning point, but a little brown is okay. Add the onions, cover and cook until the onions have produced juice and are quite tender—at least for 1 hour, but longer if you have time. I sometimes start this at nine o'clock in the morning and finish it at three o'clock in the afternoon. Obviously you must use the merest amount of heat to do it this way.

To finish, turn up the heat and reduce the liquid until the onions have begun to brown a little. You will need to be stirring constantly, so don't try to do anything else at the same time. At the last minute add the thyme and pepper to taste. (The side meat will probably have made the onions sufficiently salty.)

I put these onions between a fried pork cutlet and a sunny side up egg, and serve with a side of Mashed Rutabagas (page 42).

CHEESE PORK WITH MADEIRA SAUCE

DESPITE WHATEVER I may have tried to call this, it is always known as cheese pork. It now appears on the menu as such. You can either buy a boned pork loin and slice it into six-ounce portions or buy bone in pork chops. The bone in pork will be a little harder to pound out but will look quite elegant at the table.

Serves 6

1 2–3 pound piece of boned pork loin or 6 pork loin chops,
    about ½ an inch thick

3 large eggs

3 tablespoons milk

1 cup all-purpose flour

3 cups shredded Swiss cheese

1 teaspoon salt

½ teaspoon freshly ground black pepper

4 tablespoons (½ stick) clarified unsalted butter

Madeira Sauce (page 93)

The pork loin will be cylindrical in shape. Simply slice it into half-inch rounds with a sharp knife. Place each slice between pieces of parchment and flatten on a sturdy counter with the meat pounder. The cutlets should be an eighth of an inch thick. Pounding will make them considerably larger. For the bone in chops, partially detach a half an inch of the meat from the rib end of the bone before you flatten it between the pieces of parchment. Obviously you have to aim the meat pounder a little more carefully if there is a bone.

Beat the eggs and milk together in a shallow pan. Stir the flour, cheese, salt, and pepper together in another shallow pan. Dip the cutlets into the egg wash and then coat them with the flour-and-cheese mixture. Use the parchment to press the coating onto the meat. Fry over high heat in hot clarified butter until pretty and brown on both sides. This sounds like it would make a big mess, but it doesn't. Drain on a clean kitchen towel. Serve with a few spoonfuls of Madeira Sauce on each cutlet.

MADEIRA SAUCE

Makes about 2 cups

2 large shallots, peeled and minced

1 cup dry white wine

1½ cups freshly squeezed orange juice

1 cup Madeira

2 cups heavy cream

1 tablespoon unsalted butter

Put the shallots and wine in a shallow saucepan and reduce until almost dry, 3–4 minutes, but don't let them brown. Add the orange juice and ½ cup of the Madeira. Reduce by half, about 15 minutes. Add the cream and reduce until it begins to thicken, perhaps 10 minutes more. Add the rest of the Madeira and reduce again until thicker than before, another 10 minutes. It should coat the back of a spoon. Strain through a sieve to remove the shallots. This whole process takes time, but happily you can make this sauce days in advance. Reheat at serving time. To enrich the sauce and make it more lustrous, swirl in the butter at the last second. If you find this sauce too rich, you can replace a portion of the cream with an equal amount of good chicken stock.

I serve this with Mashed Rutabagas (page 42) and Wilted Spinach (page 115).

MEAT LOAF WITH MUSHROOM GRAVY

Cooking sometimes brings out the wily French/Southern grandmother that lurks in my soul and causes me to try to use every speck of everything. I'm likely to make this when we're cutting pork and steaks at the same time and I have good trimmings to grind up. I try to use at least 30 percent pork but as much as 50 percent is fine (though I rarely measure at all). Most butchers can provide ground pork as well as ground beef, and grocery stores often sell something called meat loaf mix that approximates this formula.

Serves 4–6

2 teaspoons salt

3 tablespoons onion powder

3 tablespoons chopped fresh parsley

2 pounds ground beef

1 pound ground pork

¼ cup freshly squeezed lemon juice

12 tablespoons (1½ sticks) unsalted butter, softened

1 cup Brown Stock (page 13) or Chicken Stock (page 15),
    or low-sodium canned

Mushroom Gravy (page 96)

Preheat oven to 375° F. Mix the salt, onion powder, and parsley together and then mix this into the ground meat. When the parsley is thoroughly distributed throughout, you can assume that the seasonings are as well. Pour the lemon juice over the meat and then—here's the good part—work in the softened butter. This takes patience because the cold meat will make the butter reharden. Just work fast. Fry up a small patty of the meat to make sure that it is seasoned correctly. Pack the meat in a standard 9 × 5-inch loaf pan, pressing down hard to get rid of any air pockets.

Bake uncovered in a bain-marie (a 9 × 13-inch baking pan with enough hot water to come halfway up the sides of the loaf pan). At least once during baking, baste the meat loaf with the stock. This meat loaf takes forever to cook, almost 2 hours sometimes. It should read 160° F at the center on a meat thermometer. The meat loaf will have shrunk some and produced a lot of juice. Allow it to cool for a while in this juice.

When the meat loaf is cool enough to touch, pour off and reserve this liquid, which will be the foundation for the Mushroom Gravy, but leave the meat loaf in its pan. I like to make this meat loaf a day in advance for several reasons. The juice is easier to degrease when it is cold; the meat loaf tastes better when I've been able to press it overnight under some kind of weight, giving it a better texture. A clean brick covered in plastic wrap is perfect. Serve with the gravy.

MUSHROOM GRAVY

Serves about 6

1½ pounds mushrooms, sliced

1 teaspoon salt

Degreased meat loaf juice

2 cups cold milk

2 tablespoons all-purpose flour

½ teaspoon freshly ground black pepper

Place the mushrooms in a heavy-bottomed 4-quart pot with a tight-fitting lid. Salt them and put them over low heat, covered. I use a heavy cast-iron

NOTE - 1 CAN EVAPORATED SKIM MILK
REMAINDER WITH MILK
3/4 CAN LOW SODIUM BEEF BROTH
DASH DRY SHERRY

skillet to weight down the lid. The idea is to prevent any moisture from escaping. The mushrooms will produce a fair amount of liquid. When they begin to float themselves, turn up the heat and add the meat loaf broth. Bring to a boil. In a jar with a top, shake together the milk and the flour until the flour is completely dissolved. Slowly whisk this into the gravy, trying not to break the boil. (If you suspect lumps, pour the milk through a sieve.) Let the gravy simmer for 10 minutes, but be careful because the flour will want to settle to the bottom and scorch. Taste for salt and add the pepper. If the gravy seems too thick, add a little more milk or stock. If it seems too thin, add a little more flour that has been combined with a little cold milk or stock. If you have made the meat loaf in advance, it may be sliced and then reheated in this sauce.

SPAGHETTI WITH MEATBALLS

Spaghetti with meatballs is an archetype. There are probably as many recipes for it as there are people who cook it. In this version, the meatballs are cooked separately and then reheated in the sauce later. This is another recipe that is a result of butchering beef and pork on the same day. You may, of course, simply buy ground meat at the store. I like a fifty-fifty ratio of beef to pork.

I learned to make the meatballs from my friend Claudia Gualtieri. She grew up in an Italian family and married an Italian man. She was of the generation in which the wife was expected to be a full-time homemaker. Whatever we may think of that custom today, it did produce some splendid cooks. Whenever I tasted anything that she sent over, even if it was a day old and wrapped in tin foil, I would always stop for a second and say to myself, "Oh yeah, this is what I'm supposed to be doing." The years of expertise were so obvious. It had all become second nature to her and often she couldn't explain just what it was she had done to make such wonderful things to eat.

Serves 6 generously

2 tablespoons olive oil

1 large onion, peeled and diced

1 large green bell pepper, cored, seeded, and diced

5 large cloves garlic, peeled and chopped

1½ pounds ground meat (either meat loaf mix or
   equal parts beef and pork)

1 28-ounce can crushed, peeled tomatoes

¼ teaspoon dried oregano

¼ teaspoon dried marjoram

1½ teaspoons dried basil

1½ teaspoons dried thyme

¼ teaspoon rosemary

¼ teaspoon sage

1 teaspoon anchovy paste

½ cup Chicken Stock (page 15), water,
    or low-sodium tomato juice

Salt (optional)

Meatballs (page 100)

1 pound fat spaghetti

Freshly grated Parmesan cheese

Heat the oil in a large heavy-bottomed pot and cook the onion and pepper until translucent but not brown, about 8 minutes. Add the garlic and sauté for a minute more. This should now smell wonderful. Add the ground meat, crumbling it as best you can. Stir constantly until the meat has browned. If this looks really greasy, pour off some of the fat but if it doesn't, don't. A little grease is good.

Add the tomatoes, all of the herbs, and the anchovy paste. I like to season heavily. You may choose to vary these amounts to suit your own tastes. In summer I might stir in chopped fresh herbs right before the sauce comes to the table. Add the stock and allow the sauce to simmer over very low heat for a while, at least 1 hour. It can bubble but not boil. Stir often.

Start out covered, but after 45 minutes remove the lid so that the sauce will thicken a bit. The larger clumps of ground meat will make excellent snacks. Canned tomatoes tend to be salty, as are the anchovies, so wait until you are almost done to decide if you need to add any salt.

Prepare the meatballs. If you make them in advance, they can be reheated in the simmering sauce. Cook the spaghetti according to the instructions on the package. Serve the meatballs and sauce over the spaghetti and top with Parmesan cheese.

MEATBALLS

6 meatballs

½ small onion, finely minced (about 3 tablespoons)
1½ pounds meat loaf mix or equal parts ground beef
   and ground pork
1½ teaspoons salt
1 tablespoon onion powder

Preheat the oven to 350° F. Combine the onion with the meat, salt, and onion powder. Form the meat into cherry-sized balls. Pat them together lightly. Do not squeeze them.

Bake the meatballs on an oiled rack on a sheet pan in a 350° F oven until they are cooked through and nicely browned, about 25 minutes. Allow them to cool a bit before you try to dislodge them from the pan. They will hold together better.

CRÈME BRÛLÉE

I RARELY HAVE time to give dinner parties anymore, but when I do, the dessert will almost certainly be either a variation of the Cashew Cake with Madame Constance's Maple Frosting (page 55) or Crème Brûlée. I had to purchase a dozen or so little half-cup ramekins for a cooking class once. Now when I entertain, I can fill all of them and bring out a whole platterful of custards at dinner's end. People can have all they want. The portions are small and so are more tempting. It's wonderful to be able to say yes to this kind of seconds. People also like to play with the blowtorch at the table and this provides enough for everyone to have a turn.

Serves 6

3 cups of heavy cream

1½ cups of half-and-half

1 split vanilla bean

9 large egg yolks

1 cup sugar

Preheat the oven to 350° F. Arrange the ramekins in a 9 × 13-inch baking dish or roasting pan and set aside.

Scald the cream and half-and-half together with the vanilla bean. Whisk together the egg yolks and sugar. When the cream begins to steam on the surface, whisk it gradually into the eggs.

Strain the mixture and divide it among six 6-ounce ramekins, saving the vanilla bean for another use or two, and pour enough hot water into the baking pan to come halfway up their sides. Bake in this bain-marie uncovered. They should become firm but still jiggly. In my small ramekins this can happen in 20 minutes, but custards are weird and will sometimes take much more time. Larger ramekins will of course take longer, so you will need to keep checking. When they are set, transfer the custards to a cooling rack for 30 minutes. Then refrigerate them, uncovered, for at least 1 hour.

At serving time dust the top with a thin layer of white sugar and brown in the broiler until the sugar has caramelized. Or do like I do, and bring a blow-torch to the table and do it on sight. Watch your fingers.

These are best eaten right away, but the caramel will hold its crunch for a few hours if you need to prepare them in advance.

*   *   *

PINEAPPLE UPSIDE-DOWN CAKE

IN NORTH CAROLINA, the seasonal fruits of winter are tropical. The first tangerines appear right before the holidays. When we were little we always found kumquats in our Christmas stockings. We had an aunt in Cuba who would sometimes ship up a case of mangoes about that time as well. It's a good time to try out recipes for lemons, bananas, coconuts, and pineapples.

One of my earliest cooking memories is of cooking a pineapple upside-down cake in a dutch oven on a campfire on a Boy Scout outing. It was made with Bisquick, and it was absolutely delicious. I was about twelve years old at the time and I could not get over this miracle. This has always been one of my favorite cakes.

FRUIT TOPPING

4 tablespoons (½ stick) unsalted butter

1 cup (packed) light brown sugar

2 tablespoons water

4–5 pineapple rings cut in halves

Maraschino cherries

½ cup pecan bits

CAKE

2 cups all-purpose flour

1 cup sugar

1 teaspoon baking powder

¼ teaspoon baking soda

¼ teaspoon salt

12 tablespoons (1½ sticks) unsalted butter, softened

¾ cup sour cream

4 large egg yolks

First, for the top of the cake: Put a large (10- or 11-inch) skillet on the eye of the stove and melt the butter. Mix the brown sugar and the water together and stir into the melting butter. Turn heat to high. When the sugar begins to melt, swirl the pan round and round until the ingredients are combined and bubbling. Make sure that the bottom of the pan is completely coated. Arrange the pineapple slices in the pan in a pretty pattern and fill in all the spaces in between with maraschino cherries and pecan pieces. Set aside.

To make the cake: Preheat the oven to 350° F. Sift together the flour, sugar, baking powder, baking soda, and salt. Beat the butter and the sour cream on medium speed in a mixer with the paddle attachment. Beat in the egg yolks. Add the dry ingredients to the butter and eggs either in the mixer if the bowl is big enough or by hand with a spatula. The batter will be fairly thick. Spread it carefully over the fruit and nuts in the skillet so as not to disrupt your design. It should be distributed evenly over the whole pan. Bake for 1 hour, but check periodically because in some ovens the top will become too brown before the cake is done. I think this is because the cast iron holds heat so well. If this seems to be happening turn the oven down to 325° F. The cake is done when the very center clearly springs back to the touch.

Allow the cake to cool just until you can handle the skillet without burning yourself. Quickly and bravely, place a large cake plate over the skillet and flip it over. The cake *should* pop out beautifully. Serve warm with fresh whipped cream.

SPRING

Springtime in Chapel Hill is beautiful. We have lots of flowering trees that bloom before they leaf out, and if we don't have a late hard frost it can be quite a show. March is also the time when the farmers' market reopens after its winter break. The market's progress can, in fact, be measured in flowers. For the first few weeks there really won't be very many things to eat—just some greens and some wintered-over root vegetables. The flowers, however, begin at once. From day one, there will be daffodils and probably little bunches of anemones. As the year unfolds, the spring bulbs and flowers that prefer cooler weather, like delphiniums and lilies, follow. There will be a week when the peonies will stop you in your tracks, followed by larkspurs, which then give way to zinnias, then sunflowers. One Wednesday you come home with an armful of tuberoses. Another time it's the alienlike celosias and so on until fall, when suddenly the dried arrangements begin to appear for holiday decorating. Edible produce unfolds in the same way, but it's always the flowers that announce each week's offering. You can see them from the road before you have even parked.

My grandmother had a wonderful backyard garden. My generation of cousins spans probably twenty years, so there were always young children around. After Mass on Easter Sunday she would hold a fairly elaborate egg hunt and brunch. All the family would come, as well as lots of friends. Catholics celebrate the end of Lent as well as the Resurrection at Easter, and she always had a large buffet with baked ham, potato salad, all kinds of little sandwiches, deviled eggs—and drinks. My grandmother's Catholicism was of the guiltless, cheery variety. St. Theresa said there was a time for penance and a time for partridges, she would remind us.

Her neighbor to the left, however, was the First Baptist Church. That congregation didn't approve of drinking at all, but especially not on a Sunday morning and not around children—loud children who could be heard over the sermon. In the South, in the 1950s, denominational differences were much more important than they are now and Catholics in a small town were viewed as strange, if not sinister, birds indeed. How my grandmother would bask in the disapproving stares of her neighbors as they left church.

Cabbage and collards have always been planted in late winter here, but recent years have seen the arrival of more exotic vegetables for spring. Leeks, celery root, and a countless variety of greens are now common. These are vegetables that can tolerate a little cold but really hate the heat of our summers. My great-grandmother would never use collards that had not been touched by frost. She wouldn't let us eat yellow corn either, but that's another season.

MINT SYRUP FOR DRINKS AND SORBET

THIS IS A SIMPLE thing we do at Crook's Corner, but people ask for this recipe as much as they do for any other. It's a syrup that we invented so that we could serve both sweetened and unsweetened tea without having to take up counter space for two separate vats.

Makes about 6 cups

4 cups sugar

4 cups water

4 cups fresh mint leaves, tightly packed

Grated zest of 2 lemons

1½ cups freshly squeezed lemon juice

Bring the sugar and water to a boil in a large nonreactive pot with a tight-fitting lid. Remove from the heat when the sugar is completely dissolved. Add the mint leaves and lemon zest, making sure that the leaves are all submerged. Cover and let them steep for at least 15 minutes. Longer is fine. Add the lemon juice and strain. Use the syrup to sweeten tea or add it to sparkling water for a spritzer. If you reduce the sugar to 2 cups, you can churn this in an ice-cream maker for a wonderful mint sorbet.

STUFFED ARTICHOKES

ARTICHOKES ARE A food that people in Louisiana eat lots of and other Southerners don't. This is a takeoff on any number of stuffed artichokes served around New Orleans. I prefer to steam artichokes as opposed to boiling them so that they will not become saturated with water. These days there is a pretty variety in the stores that is spineless and resembles a flower. Avoid these in favor of the traditional spiny variety. The new one has very little meat in its heart and also sometimes has a surprise layer of very hard leaves near the center.

Serves 6

6 large artichokes

4 lemons

½ teaspoon salt

1 teaspoon freshly ground black pepper

3 ounces goat cheese, sliced into 6 equal discs

4 cups bread crumbs

8 tablespoons (1 stick) unsalted butter, diced and very cold

1 small red onion, peeled and diced

4 tablespoons capers, drained

4 tablespoons chopped fresh parsley

1 cup whole-fat cottage cheese, rinsed and drained

¼ cup freshly grated Parmesan cheese

4 tablespoons extra-virgin olive oil

Preheat the oven to 350° F. With a serrated knife, trim the stem end of each artichoke to make it sit level and to remove any dry or discolored outer leaves. Then lop off the top of the vegetable, maybe a half an inch down. With kitchen shears, snip off the spines at the tip of each leaf. Put the artichokes in a bowl or pot large enough to contain them, and cover with water. (Actually, you will not be able to cover them because they float, but you know what I mean.) Zest the lemons. Put aside the zest, and squeeze the juice of 3 of the lemons into the water. Save the fourth lemon for later.

Fill the steamer with water and bring it to boil. Cook the artichokes in the steamer basket until a sharp knife will pass all the way through the thickest part without resistance. A fist-sized artichoke takes about 19 minutes. Be careful not to cook them to the point of mushiness. Remove the artichokes from the steamer and place them in something stainless steel or glass to cool. Never put an artichoke on aluminum.

When they are cool enough to touch, remove the choke from the heart of each artichoke. (I use a melon baller.) Stand the artichokes up in a roasting pan and sprinkle with salt and pepper. Place a disc of goat cheese in the bottom of each artichoke. In a medium-sized mixing bowl combine the bread crumbs, butter, onion, capers, lemon zest, parsley, and cottage cheese, and Parmesan cheese. Gently fill the center of the artichokes with the mixture and force as much as possible all down among the leaves as well. Sprinkle with more salt and pepper. Cut the last zested lemon in half and take six pretty slices from the centers. Squeeze the rest of the lemon over the artichokes. Rest a slice on top of each artichoke and drizzle it with the oil. Bake uncovered, for about 45 minutes, until the cheese and butter are melted and the bread crumbs have begun to brown. Serve hot.

TURTLE SOUP

I KNOW THAT turtle meat is really hard to find these days, but this soup is so good that I've included this recipe on the outside chance that you are able to. Lillian Hellman warns against trying to catch your own in *Pentimento*, but snapping turtles are raised for food in Louisiana. Some specialty food purveyors can get turtle meat for you. I also sometimes run into it at really old fish markets.

This recipe was given to me by my friend Ray Farris, sort of. It's been done from memory for so many years now that he may no longer recognize it. Ray came to work for me in the mid-1980s. He is from New Orleans and has that wonderful food sense that the natives there seem to have. When Ray came to apply for a job, he told me that he either wanted to be a chef or an investment banker. I knew I had to act.

We first began serving turtle soup at La Residence when the movie *Babette's Feast* came to town. The owner of the theater suggested that we serve that menu during the run. People would go to the movie and then walk around the corner for dinner. Babette's soup was a clear consommé with quenelles as I recall, but Ray thought that we should use a Louisiana-style soup instead. I asked him to provide the recipe. Here it is — I hope — an amalgamation of the recipes that he researched.

Ray is now an investment banker in Singapore.

Makes about 2½ quarts

2 tablespoons vegetable oil

1 medium onion, peeled and diced (about 1½ cups)

6 stalks celery, sliced

1 green bell pepper, cored, seeded, and diced

1 pound ground beef

2 pounds ground turtle meat

5 cloves garlic, peeled and minced

1 28-ounce can fancy-style, chopped, peeled tomatoes

4 cups Chicken Stock (page 15)

4 tablespoons (½ stick) unsalted butter

½ cup all-purpose flour

5 bay leaves

½ teaspoon dried red pepper flakes

1 teaspoon whole cloves

1 teaspoon whole allspice

1½ teaspoons each of dried basil

1½ teaspoons dried thyme

1½ teaspoons dried marjoram

2 teaspoons salt

1 teaspoon freshly ground black pepper

3 hard-boiled eggs, chopped

Juice of 1 lemon

¼ cup chopped fresh parsley

Water (if needed)

Sherry or Madeira, for garnish

Heat the oil in a large soup pot. Add the onion, celery, and pepper, and sauté until they begin to soften, about 10 minutes. Add the ground meats and cook until brown. If this appears too greasy, strain, reserving the liquid, and return to the pot. Add the garlic. Cook 1–2 minutes more and add the tomatoes and Stock. Cover and simmer on low heat while you make the roux.

Soften the butter in a skillet and stir in the flour until you have a thick paste. Turn up the heat and stir until the roux is the color of peanut butter.

Remove from the heat at once and allow to cool a minute. When the roux has firmed a bit, pour off any excess fat that has separated out from it. Stir the roux into the simmering soup, making sure that it doesn't fall to the bottom of the pot in a clump, or it will scorch. Allow the soup to come to a gentle boil and then, again, remove as much of the fat as possible.

Now add all the bay leaves, pepper flakes, whole cloves, whole allspice, basil, thyme, marjoram, salt, and pepper. If the soup seems too thick, add a little water. The thickness will vary according to the liquid in the tomatoes and the juiciness of the other vegetables. The tomatoes will also determine how much salt you will need to add.

The soup should simmer for at least 1 hour, longer if possible. At the last minute add the eggs, lemon juice, and parsley. Taste again for salt and pepper. Serve with a splash of good sherry or Madeira in the bottom of each bowl.

WILTED SPINACH

I USE WILTED spinach with everything, at least until the weather gets too hot. Spinach cooks down to nothing in no time, so you need to act quickly as if preparing a stir fry. To test this recipe I bought a ten-ounce bag of fresh, pre-washed spinach from my grocer. That made four generous servings, all of which I ate for breakfast—it was early morning at the time. Unless spinach is especially stalky, I don't remove the stems anymore. I like their texture. When Hong first came to work for me she was astounded that we discarded those, especially if they were from the red-stemmed variety. "Best part!" she would insist and gather them up to make soup.

Serves 4

½ cup water

2 tablespoons unsalted butter

10 ounces spinach

½ teaspoon salt

Put the water in a large skillet (or a wok) over high heat. If you have bought spinach that requires washing, reduce the amount of water in the skillet, since some water will cling to the leaves. When the water begins to bubble, add half of the butter. Add as much spinach as will fit and toss about with tongs. As quickly as possible add the rest of the spinach. The spinach should be hot and just barely collapsed. Total cooking time should be 3 minutes, start to finish. Toss in the rest of the butter and the salt. Serve at once, draining briefly as you do.

A COLLECTION OF WILTED SALADS

YEARS AGO IN PARIS, my friend Nancy Brown and I used to go for lunch in a tiny, crowded, smoky wine bar on the quai des Grands Augustins. It was just two or three steps from the river. In warm weather the whole front could be opened up. The ceiling was low, so it felt like you were on a boat. We would go there for the wilted *salade aux lardons*. The business of this place was wine, so the kitchen consisted of a hot plate and a toaster oven.

This delicious salad was crowned with a tiny whole goat cheese that is known as a *crottin*. The cheese has a brielike rind and a center that becomes soft and gooey when warmed. It was dressed with browned diced fatback that had been tossed with its own grease and some vinegar.

This is pretty much the procedure for all wilted salads. Sturdy, often bitter greens provide the base of the salad. Something fancy is placed on top and then some kind of hot salty grease mixed with vinegar is poured over everything.

Two years ago, the people at Chapel Hill Creamery began making their own cows' milk *crottins*, so I've been able to offer this delicious salad here in North Carolina. In the fall I sometimes expand it into a main course by tucking wilted spinach, sautéed green beans, grilled fennel, and Mashed Rutabagas (page 42) around the sides.

I've included two more salads here, since the procedure is the same for all. One uses Salt-Cured Duck Legs (page 47) and one uses shad roe. The preparation of the greens is the same for all three.

GREENS FOR WILTED SALADS

Serves 4–6

1 large or 2 small heads of frisée or escarole

4 Belgian endives

1 head radicchio

The frisée or escarole will need to be trimmed, washed, and drained. It is usually sufficient just to remove the outside leaves of the endive and radicchio. This can either be assembled on a large platter or on individual salad plates.

Break the radicchio apart. Use the larger outside leaves to line the plate. Shred the small center leaves and toss with the frisée. Remove the larger outside leaves from the endives and arrange them in a star pattern on top of the radicchio. Cut the smaller center leaves into round and set aside. Put the frisée in the center of the endive stars and sprinkle the chopped endive on top. The salad is now ready to dress.

WARM CROTTIN SALAD

Serves 4

1 tablespoon dried cherries

½ cup red wine vinegar

4 *crottin*s

4 tablespoons (½ stick) unsalted butter

½ cup pecan pieces

½ cup chopped scallions (white and green parts)

Preheat the oven to 350° F. A toaster oven works well for this. Do not use a microwave. In a small saucepan over low heat or in a microwave, warm the cherries in the vinegar. Allow to steep for at least 30 minutes. Discard the cherries.

Place the *crottins* on an oiled baking sheet and put in the oven to warm through, 3–5 minutes depending on the thickness. Carefully slide them onto the salad greens.

Put the butter in a small sauté pan over high heat. Swirl it around for 30 seconds to melt. Add the pecans and continue to swirl the pan for about 3 minutes until the nuts begin to smell toasty. Add the scallions and the vinegar all at once and pour over the salad.

WILTED SALAD WITH SALT-CURED DUCK LEGS

Serves 4–6

3 Salt-Cured Duck Legs (page 47)

1 tablespoon dried cherries

½ cup red wine vinegar

4 tablespoons (½ stick) unsalted butter

½ cup pecan pieces

¼ cup chopped scallions (white and green parts)

Shred the duck meat off of the bone and arrange on top of salad greens.

In a small saucepan over low heat or in a microwave, warm the cherries in the vinegar. Allow to steep for at least 30 minutes. Discard or eat the cherries.

Put the butter in a small sauté pan over high heat. Swirl it around for 30 seconds to melt. Add the pecans and continue to swirl the pan for about 3 minutes until the nuts begin to smell toasty. Add the scallions and then add the vinegar all at once and pour over the salad.

WILTED SALAD WITH SHAD ROE

Serves 4

4 pairs of shad roe

Ice water

½ pound side meat or pancetta

1 cup all-purpose flour

¼ teaspoon salt

½ small red onion, peeled and cut into strips

4 tablespoons lemon juice

½ teaspoon freshly ground black pepper

Rinse the pairs of shad roe and soak them in ice water to firm them up. They are encased in a membrane that you want to leave intact, but sometimes there are extraneous veins and connective tissue that you should try to carefully remove. Dice and render the side meat, reserving both the meat and the grease.

Heat the grease in a large skillet over medium-high heat. If it seems a little skimpy you may augment it with butter or oil. Mix together the flour and salt. Prick the shad roe sacks a few times on both sides with a straight pin. Dredge them in the flour and shake off the excess. Fry in the grease, turning once, carefully, about 3 minutes on the first side and 2 minutes on the second. They will brown a little. Be careful because sometimes they will pop. When they are hot through, place them on the salad greens.

Quickly add the side meat and the onion to the pan and toss to warm. The onions should remain almost raw. Add the lemon juice and pepper and pour over the salad.

CARROT SLAW

THIS RECIPE CAME from the French grandmother of a friend. I like to serve it with fried seafood. This fresh, citrusy side dish is a perfect foil for the browned butter sauce I like on the crabs. For Soft-Shelled Crabs (page 129), I pair the carrot slaw with slaw made from purple cabbage. The colors on the plate are quite startling.

Makes about 3 cups

3 large cloves garlic, peeled

5 carrots, peeled and sliced (about 1½ pounds)

1 lemon

¼ teaspoon salt

¼ teaspoon sugar

2 tablespoons extra-virgin olive oil

Bruise the garlic and toss it with the sliced carrots in a large bowl. Zest the lemon and then quarter it. Add the zest and all of the lemon pulp, minus the seeds, to the carrots. Dust with the salt and sugar. Toss together and allow to stand for half an hour. The carrots will produce a bit of juice. Put everything—juice too—in the bowl of a food processor. Pulse to grind coarsely to the consistency of slaw. Stir in the oil. Taste for salt and sweetness. This will keep for about a week in the refrigerator.

POTATO SALAD

THERE ARE THREE kinds of people in the world. One kind believes that there is only one recipe for potato salad. Probably the one that Mama used. Another can't wait to try the next new recipe for potato salad. The third acknowledges that there are many kinds of potato salad but really only likes the one Mama made. This third group holds the balance of power. This is not a family recipe but one developed over time and motivated by a love of grease and salt.

This potato salad is good cold, but it is really good while still warm. I deliberately cut the potatoes into different-sized pieces so that some of them will mash up while others remain in chunks.

Serves 4–6

2½ pounds potatoes, peeled and cut into uneven chunks

3 teaspoons salt

½ cup Hellmann's or other good-quality mayonnaise

¼ cup French's Ballpark or your favorite salad mustard

½ cup sweet pickle relish or chowchow with some of its juice

8 slices bacon rendered, drained, and diced

1 teaspoon whole celery seeds

1 bunch scallions (white and green parts), trimmed and chopped

1 tablespoon chopped fresh parsley

Put the potatoes in a 3-quart saucepan and cover with 2 inches of water. Add 2 teaspoons of the salt. Bring to a boil and cook until the larger pieces can be easily pierced through with a fork. Drain the potatoes in a colander and allow them to sit until they are dried a little by their own heat.

Transfer to a large bowl, and while still warm add the mustard and mayonnaise. Stir vigorously for a minute to mash up the smaller pieces, and then fold in everything else.

MY MASHED POTATOES

I DON'T LIKE "whipped" potatoes. If they are too smooth and creamy, they begin to resemble instant. I deliberately leave mine a little chunky. I also hate potatoes without enough salt. You can suit yourself.

Serves 4–6

4 pounds baking potatoes

3 quarts cold water

½ tablespoon salt

6 tablespoons (¾ stick) unsalted butter

½–1 teaspoon minced garlic

½ cup heavy cream

½ teaspoon freshly ground black pepper

Peel the potatoes and cut them into rough inch-sized chunks. Put them in a nonaluminum pot in enough cold water to cover by 2 inches. Add the salt. Bring to a boil uncovered over high heat. When the water comes to a full boil, about 15 minutes, the potatoes will be close to done. While you are waiting for the potatoes to cook, melt 4 tablespoons of the butter together with the garlic in a small saucepan or in the microwave.

Test the potatoes. They should be crumbly to the touch but not completely mushy. Drain them in a colander and let them sit for a minute or two so that they will dry out a little from their own heat.

Mash them by hand—no electric devices please—with the melted butter and garlic. Fold in the cream and the pepper. Taste for salt and add more if you need to. If they seem too dry, stir in a little more cream. Dot the top with the remaining 2 tablespoons of the butter and serve at once.

SAUTÉED LEEKS AND CABBAGE

THERE IS AN Indian restaurant in town that always has cabbage sautéed with caraway seeds on its buffet. Every time I go there I am reminded of how much I loved what my mother always called fried cabbage when I was growing up. It finally dawned on me that I too could have fried cabbage on my menu if I wanted. I decided that leeks might be good in combination with the cabbage.

Serves 4–6

2 large leeks

1 very small green cabbage

2 tablespoons (¼ stick) unsalted butter

1 teaspoon salt

½ teaspoon freshly ground black pepper

This could not be simpler. Trim and peel the leeks and cut them into 2-inch lengths. Then cut the pieces into matchstick-sized strips. Since leeks are always sandy, submerge them in cold water and let them soak for a while. Then quarter the cabbage and remove the core. Slice thinly across the leaves. I am always amazed at the amount of food there is in one cabbage. Drain the leeks—they don't have to be dry—and toss with the cabbage. Quickly sauté in butter with salt and pepper. The cabbage should be mostly cooked but still a little crunchy.

FRIED BLUEFISH WITH POTATOES, SIDE MEAT, VEGETABLES, AND FRESH HERBS

Bluefish is my favorite fried fish. Sometimes customers comment that it tastes like fish (I always explain that it *is* fish), but that is why I like it. Bluefish migrate up and down North Carolina's coast every year so we get two seasons of them. This recipe is a true example of grandmother meets *grand-mère* in that it combines this local favorite with a technique referred to in France as *à la bonne-femme*. I further this along by tossing in a handful of *fines herbes* in at the last minute. This recipe is even more appealing because it is a whole meal (fish, vegetable, and potatoes) in one pan.

Serves 6

3 pounds baking potatoes

3 quarts of water

3 teaspoons salt

½ pound side meat, bacon, or pancetta

1 medium red onion, peeled and diced

4 stalks of celery, washed and diced

1 cup all-purpose flour

½ teaspoon freshly ground black pepper

6 bluefish fillets (6–8 ounces each)

2–3 tablespoons unsalted butter

3 tablespoons apple cider vinegar

2 tablespoons coarsely chopped fresh parsley

2 tablespoons coarsely chopped fresh tarragon

1 tablespoon coarsely chopped fresh chervil

1 tablespoon snipped fresh chives

Peel the potatoes and cut them into a quarter-inch dice (imagine cutting french fries into cubes). Submerge them in cool water. Bring the 3 quarts of water to a boil with 2 teaspoons of the salt. Blanch the potatoes until done but still crisp and then refresh under cool running water. Drain and set aside.

Dice the side meat and render in a skillet until brown. Reserve the meat and the grease separately.

Mix the onion and celery together in a medium-sized bowl.

Season the flour with the pepper and the remaining teaspoon of the salt. Pat the fish dry. Put the side meat grease in a large skillet on medium-high heat. Dredge the fish in the flour and fry it, uncrowded, 3–4 minutes on each side until done through and pretty and brown. Transfer the fish either to individual plates or to a large serving platter.

Wipe out the skillet and add the butter over medium-high heat. As soon as the butter begins to sputter, add the potatoes. Cook 4 minutes, shaking the pan until they begin to brown a little. Add the side meat. Cook 3 more minutes and then add the celery and onions. Continue stirring or tossing the pan for 2 minutes more. These last vegetables should remain a little bit crunchy. Turn the heat to high. Cook 2 minutes more then add the vinegar all at once. Remove from heat and stir in the herbs. Pour over the fish and serve at once. The wonderful aroma will fill the dining room.

QUICK JAMBALAYA

ORDINARILY, JAMBALAYA IS baked for a few hours, but once I was asked to teach a class on the food of Louisiana, and class time would not allow for this. I developed this recipe, which is actually a kind of risotto made from the rice that the Mexican men who work for me often make for lunch.

1 whole velvetized chicken (about 3 pounds) (see page 15)

4 cups Chicken Stock (page 15)

12 ounces spicy link-sausage, sliced, and/or bulk sausage, crumbled

3 ounces side meat, bacon, or pancetta, diced (about ½ cup)

1 small onion, peeled and diced (about 1 cup)

3 stalks celery, diced (about 1 cup)

1 large green bell pepper, cored, seeded, and diced (about 1 cup)

6 ounces fresh or frozen okra, cut into ½-inch slices (about 2 cups)

1 tablespoon vegetable oil (optional)

1 cup uncooked long grain rice

3 cloves garlic, peeled and minced (about 3 teaspoons)

⅛ teaspoon dried red pepper flakes

¾ teaspoon dried basil

¾ teaspoon dried marjoram

1 bay leaf

⅛ teaspoon cayenne pepper

1 14.5-ounce canned diced tomatoes

½ teaspoon Tabasco or other hot pepper sauce

1½ pounds shrimp and/or oysters, shelled and cleaned (optional)

Salt

Pick the meat from the velvetized chicken and set aside. Return the skin and bones to the stock to enrich it and reduce it to about 4 cups, strained and degreased. The reduction will take about 30 minutes. Keep the stock on a low simmer.

Brown the side meat and sausage in a large, heavy-bottomed pot. Remove the meat and sauté onion, celery, and bell pepper in the sausage grease until translucent. Remove the vegetables. Add the oil, if needed, and brown the raw rice in the same pan. When the rice begins to resemble Rice Krispies, add the garlic and pepper flakes, basil, marjoram, bay leaf, and cayenne, stirring constantly. When the garlic begins to smell cooked, about 1 minute, add the tomatoes, juice and all, and the okra. Follow with 2 cups of the stock. Stir constantly. The rice will begin to absorb the liquid. Add a little more stock if the rice begins to look dry. Keep stirring until the rice appears halfway done, about 18 minutes. Add the vegetables and sausage. Keep stirring and again add stock as it is absorbed, about 8 minutes more. When the rice seems almost ready, add the picked chicken. Sometimes I use shellfish—shrimp or oysters—in this recipe. They can be added at this time as well. Finish the rice by stirring and adding more broth if needed. Finally, stir in a few shakes of the Tabasco and taste for salt. Cover and let the jambalaya rest for 10 minutes before serving.

SAUTÉED CHICKEN LIVERS WITH ONIONS AND BROWN SAUCE

IT'S HARD TO imagine serving liver at a dinner party, but it definitely has its aficionados. We give these chicken livers a couple of runs a year at Crook's Corner, and they are greeted each time with great delight.

Serves 4

2 pounds chicken livers

1 cup super-refined sauce flour such as Wondra or Shake & Blend

1 teaspoon salt

¾ teaspoon pepper

4 tablespoons bacon grease

1 medium onion, peeled, halved, and sliced lengthwise

1 large medium-ripe avocado, peeled, pitted, and cut into ½ inch strips

3 tablespoons Bourbon Brown Sauce (page 171)

Let the livers sit in a colander for a minute or two to drain thoroughly. Season the flour with the salt and pepper. Melt the bacon grease in a large frying pan over medium-high heat. Toss the livers in the flour and shake off the excess. Fry the livers, uncrowded, in the bacon grease, turning once, 2 minutes to a side. I like them a little pink in the center, but you can of course cook them longer if you prefer. Add the onion and toss everything together. Cook the onion for 3 minutes or so. It should wilt a little but retain some crunch. If there seems to be excess grease, pour it off at this time. Turn the heat to high and add the Brown Sauce (page 171). Reduce the sauce for 1½ minutes. Fold in the avocado and let it warm through for 30 seconds. Serve at once with rice and wilted spinach (page 115).

SOFT-SHELLED CRABS

YEARS AGO WHILE I was briefly toying with the concept of vegetarianism, a friend showed up at my house with a cooler full of live soft-shelled crabs from Maryland. I stared down at them wriggling in my sink, came to the conclusion that it was impossible to return them to the sea, and dispatched them forthwith. I've never looked back. This recipe was arrived at by committee one spring long ago in the kitchen of La Residence. In North Carolina, the soft-shelled crab season traditionally begins with the full moon in May. The staff had been debating the nuances of crab cooking and this is what we came up with.

Serves 4

8 fresh soft-shelled crabs

1 cup self-rising flour

1 cup Maseca instant corn masa mix

1 teaspoon salt

½ teaspoon freshly ground black pepper

1 cup buttermilk

½ cup clarified unsalted butter

3 tablespoons unsalted butter

4 tablespoons chopped garlic

Juice of 1 lemon (about ¼ cup)

¼ cup thin basil chiffonade

Clean the crabs (if your seafood market won't do it for you) by first snipping off the face with kitchen shears. They should be soft and squishy all over. Then lift up each side of the carapace and snip out the gills. (These are four or five white, curved, pointed "devil's fingers" extending from the center of the crab to the edges of the shell on both sides.) Flip the crab over and cut off the tail flap—on males it is narrow; on females it is fat. Hold the crab under cool running water and gently squeeze out the yellow guts that are inside and just under the top of the shell. You don't need to squeeze the main part of the body beneath this shell. Rinse thoroughly and pat dry. Very appetizing so far, yes?

Mix the flour and Maseca together and season with the salt and pepper. It is very important to use enough salt, so taste the flour before you begin.

Dip the crabs in buttermilk and the dredge in the flour. Shake off any excess flour and sauté them in very hot clarified butter—a quarter inch deep—until pretty and brown, turning once. The crabs should be crispy and very hot at the center. Remove them to a warm platter. Be careful, because they pop and spit a great deal, especially when very fresh. My staff refers to this as frying fire crackers.

Pour off the butter, but try to keep as much of the crumbs and browned flour in the pan as possible. Put the pan back on high heat and add the 3 tablespoons of whole butter. Begin swirling the pan at once. The butter will begin to melt and smell toasty. When the butter is pretty and brown, quickly add the garlic, swirl to spread it around, and immediately add the lemon juice to prevent the garlic from browning. Remove from the heat, add the basil, and pour over the crabs. Serve at once. (They are not good cold.)

This process sounds tricky, but once you have done it correctly it will always be easy because the smell is so divine it will guide you ever after. I serve these with Carrot Slaw (page 120).

CRAB STEW

ALTHOUGH THIS IS one of my favorite foods from childhood, I have never served it at a restaurant. It is far too messy. My grandmother would make us go outside to eat it. The picnic table would be covered with newspaper and each place would be set with a nutcracker as well as silverware. After dinner the shells would be rolled up in the newspaper and taken straight to the trash can.

Serves 4–6

12 blue crabs

½ cup diced side meat

1 tablespoon unsalted butter

2 medium onions, peeled and diced

1 pound potatoes, peeled and quartered

1 teaspoon salt

1 teaspoon freshly ground black pepper

½ teaspoon dried red pepper flakes

2–3 bay leaves

¼ cup all-purpose flour

1 cup cold milk

Water

6–12 slices country-style white bread

Crabs must always be bought live. Unless you have a fish market that will clean them for you, you must dress them yourself. Be careful because they will try to pinch you. It's best to do this quickly. Flip them one by one onto their backs. There is a dividing line in the shell that runs from face to tail. If you slam them on the counter hard when you flip them over, they will be stunned enough to stop wiggling for a second, giving you the opportunity to take aim and split them down the middle with the blow of a heavy butcher knife. Pop off the carapace (now in two pieces) and rinse under cool water, using your hands to scrape away the yellow "devil's fingers," or "deadman's bones." I guess you aren't supposed to eat this.

Brown the side meat in a large soup pot to render its grease and to brown a little. Add the butter and the onions and toss to coat. Let this return to a sizzle. Add the potatoes and crab halves and cover with water. Season with the salt, pepper, and pepper flakes. Taste periodically and adjust the seasoning to your taste. (I like to season heavily.) Add the bay leaves. Bring to a boil and reduce to a simmer at once. Cook for about 30 minutes. The potatoes should be falling apart.

In a jar with a lid, shake together the flour with the milk. When it is completely combined, pour it through a sieve into the simmering stew. Stir well so that the flour doesn't sink to the bottom and scorch. Turn up the heat a little and cook for 15 more minutes. If too thick, thin with a little more milk.

Line big soup bowls with slices of white bread and fill with stew. You pretty much have to pick the crabs apart with your fingers, so you will need nutcrackers and lots of napkins. Have extra bread handy.

How They Landed at Crooks

You can wash dishes in any language. For that reason, the restaurant kitchen is often the first stop for new immigrants looking for work. My first group, back in the early 1970s, was from Vietnam. Church groups here in Chapel Hill were helping to resettle the refugees and line up jobs for them. At first we hired the occasional single man. Then we got Mia and Hong. They stayed more than 15 years.

Hong Nguyen is still one of my best friends. Over the years I have learned more from her than from almost anyone I can name. I remember when she and her husband, Mia Bu Lam, first came to La Residence. In her arms was a squirmy five-year-old named Ton. Hong has never learned English very well. She wasn't literate in her own language either, but Ton now speaks the English of Gomer Pyle. First-generation immigrants rarely have time to study languages—they have too many jobs—but their children learn quickly. Much of Hong's life had been completely chaotic, but she always maintained a tiny space of formality and propriety whatever her circumstances. The terrible apartments in the bad neighborhoods where they first lived were always spotless. There was always a shrine, always some flowers. The family considered itself very lucky and was always grateful for what they had. From Hong I learned the value and dignity of those people who must do menial work. That being uneducated has nothing to do with innate intelligence. Terrible things had happened to her, but she always went forward, chin up and ready to deal with whatever might come next. Hong is a great cook with a great sense of humor. She is fun to tease. I taught myself to drink a glass of olive oil over ice just so I could see the expression on her face. I went to her son's wedding and her husband's funeral. Her son became an excellent mechanic and, remarkably, despite being raised here, married a woman that his mother picked out on a return visit to Vietnam. Now that Hong is an elderly grandmother, she has given herself permission to quit working and to live with her son and his family.

Between then and now I've hired Chinese graduate students afraid to go home after Tiananmen Square, a few Eastern Europeans before the collapse of the Soviet Union, and the occasional Central American. "Willy" (he chose an English name) finally returned to Shanghai where he has become a tycoon. I still see him when he comes to town. Ladislav, alas, returned to Brno and I've lost track of him.

Today most of the kitchen staff comes from Mexico. They're here under circumstances different from Hong's, but their admirable qualities are the same: people who work hard and who have gone through a great deal to get here. They've brought me great food and music—nopales and Molotov. I've worked with them for about ten years, enough time now that half of my vacations are spent in central Mexico visiting former staff members who have returned home. When they leave here, they always shake my hand and say, "Thank you for the work."

I realize that everyone in the world cannot come to live here in the United States, but it's hard to imagine that the people who complain so loudly about immigration have had much experience with new immigrants. Getting to know people from all these places has been one of the great privileges of my life.

BAKED HAM FOR A BIG BRUNCH

"When I get done, I want to be able to make a ham sandwich," I said.

"Then you want a tenderized ham. Cook it just like it says on the wrapper." This was my exchange with Cliff Collins, who owns our local meat market, the first time I attempted this dish. When the ham arrived, the wrapper said "fully cooked." I forged ahead. Yes, a tenderized ham is fully cooked, and I suppose that it would make a fine ham sandwich, but the twice-cooked glazed ham that it becomes turns people into gluttons, standing around the platter long after the meal is over.

Serves a crowd

1 tenderized ham (about 18 pounds)
1 cup (packed) light brown sugar
½ cup Dijon mustard
¼ cup Grade B pure maple syrup

This recipe could not be simpler. Get a tenderized ham from your butcher. It's hard to get a small one, so save this for a crowd or a week at the beach. Cook it, covered, like it says on the wrapper. Usually it will say 20–25 minutes per pound at 325° F. You are talking an easy 7 hours here. Put an inch of water in the bottom of the roasting pan. The ham should be on a rack. If you have to use foil to cover the ham, put a piece of buttered kitchen parchment between the ham and the foil.

Uncover the ham for the last hour of cooking. Lift off the carapace of skin that covers the top of the ham. It will usually come off in one piece. Tuck it beside the ham. It will turn into cracklins. Scrape away some of the fat that will be revealed when you removed the skin. It will be all melted, so this can be easily done with a dinner knife. Make a paste of the sugar, mustard, and maple syrup, and coat the ham with it. This will run everywhere and make a mess, but that's okay. Baste with the pan juices at least once during this period. The ham is ready when it is all but falling off of the bone and is a minimum of 165° F at the center. It needs to sit at least 1 hour after cooking before it can be sliced.

HONEYSUCKLE SORBET

THERE WAS AN old run-down house next door to Crook's Corner where we had an office. In the yard was a huge mound of honeysuckle that bloomed every summer, almost stifling us with its perfume. Anyone who has grown up in the South knows what I'm talking about. Particularly on hot nights, the smell is everywhere. As children, we were taught to suck that one tiny drop of nectar out of the neck of each flower. When people taste this sorbet, they ask me incredulously if I squeeze that little drop out of each flower. I don't. When my boss Gene Hamer asked me if I could turn the honeysuckle into food, I was doubtful because most flowers don't taste good; sweet-smelling ones tend to taste bitter. But I remembered reading somewhere that the Arabs in Spain and Sicily had once made flower ices, so I tracked down some old recipes. Since I expected it to be awful, I only made a little bit the first time.

The first bite of this tends to silence people, particularly if they grew up around here. It's like walking around at night with your mouth open. In fact, the flowers are best if picked at night because that is when they really release their fragrance. I used to put a Budweiser in each pocket and go out picking each night after work. The best flowers seem to be the wild ones with the pink- ish throats, although the regular ivory-colored ones are fine. Hybrid cultivars are useless, and don't pick flowers from busy roadsides or the sorbet may taste sooty. You have to remove all the leaves that invariably get mixed up in the flowers or you will taste the chlorophyll.

Makes about 2 quarts

4 cups (tightly packed but not smashed) honeysuckle flowers,
    leaves and stems discarded

5⅓ cups cool water

1⅓ cups water

2 cups sugar

Few drops of freshly squeezed lemon juice

Speck of cinnamon

Place the flowers in a nonreactive container (glass or stainless steel) and cover with the cool water. Weight down with a plate. Let them stand on the counter overnight.

In a small saucepan make a syrup out of the sugar and water by boiling it until all the sugar is dissolved and it begins to look lustrous and slightly thick, 3–5 minutes. Add a few drops of lemon juice to prevent the sugar from recrystallizing. Cool the syrup completely. Strain the honeysuckle infusion, gently pressing the blossoms so as not to waste any of your previous efforts. Combine the two liquids and add the merest dusting of cinnamon. You don't want to taste it but you can tell if it's not there. I use the tip of a sharp boning knife to measure it. Churn in an ice-cream maker. This does not keep for more than a week or two.

MAYHAW SORBET

I BUY A LOT of produce from the sisters Mary Andrews and Blanche Norwood, stuff that you could never get from an ordinary supplier: wild persimmons, Jerusalem artichokes, fresh figs by the gallon, perfect fresh pecan halves, and occasionally mayhaws. The mayhaw, also called the May cherry here in North Carolina, is a wild semisweet fruit that resembles a tiny crab apple. This is what I call a wish and a prayer recipe because the fruit is different every year, so you must rely on a certain amount of observation each time you make it. I think we must be at the northern edge of its habitat here in North Carolina, because some years we get none at all owing to late freezes. I understand that they are quite common in Texas and Louisiana.

Makes about 2 quarts

8 pounds mayhaws
1 cup sugar
2 tablespoons light corn syrup
Dash of freshly squeezed lemon juice
Water

You have to do this by taste. The last time I had 8 pounds of mayhaws I tossed them with enough sugar to coat them lightly, put them in a stainless steel bowl, and gently bruised them with a potato masher. Then I let them sit for a few hours. Mayhaws are mostly seeds and pureeing them is a real pain. It seems to me that the best method is to use a heavy cone-shaped colander and its matching *champignon*, or pestle. Produce as much pulp as you have patience for. Then add the corn syrup and a dash of lemon juice. Taste. Does this taste like it's going to be delicious sorbet? The puree will probably need a little bit of additional liquid. If it seems too sour, add a little sugar syrup made by boiling equal parts of sugar and water together. If it seems too sweet, just add plain water. I always add a little lemon juice, even to sour fruits, because it seems to brighten the sorbet. This is never the same from batch to batch because the ripeness of the fruit dictates the amount of natural sugars and moisture present.

Load the mixture into an ice-cream maker and churn. After what seems like a reasonable amount of time, check to see if it is setting up. If it is, taste to see if it is still sweet enough. You can still add a little more sugar syrup. If it is not setting up, you have too much sugar for the volume of puree and will need to add more water. Start with ½ cup and check for success after 15 minutes. You will be able to tell when you have it right because the sorbet will begin to freeze right away. This may seem like a lot of trouble, but once you've been successful it becomes a cinch. It's worth it. After honeysuckle sorbet, mayhaw sorbet produces the most comment.

BIG BISCUIT PUDDING WITH RASPBERRY SAUCE AND WHIPPED CREAM

THIS RECIPE WAS added at the last minute at the request of my editor. I explained that it really isn't a recipe, because it changes every time I make it. Its ingredients are all leftovers from Sunday brunch. It then occurred to me that this might present a truer picture of how I *actually* cook. In other words, even though I've written a cookbook, I rarely use recipes myself anymore. I insisted that I not be required to give a recipe for day-old biscuits.

Serves 12

2 cups half-and-half

3 allspice berries

1 cinnamon stick

2 pieces star anise

2 tablespoons fresh ginger, grated

1 vanilla bean

1 tablespoon unsalted butter, softened

1½ cups raspberry jam

1 cup orange juice

8–10 day-old biscuits (depending on size)

15 large eggs, beaten

¼ cup milk

1½ cups sugar

Fresh whipped cream

Scald the half-and-half in a saucepan with the allspice, cinnamon, star anise, the ginger, and vanilla. Set aside for at least 30 minutes to steep. Butter a 9 × 12 × 4 baking dish (use about ½ tablespoon). In another sauce pan melt 3 cups of the jelly (I often use raspberry) with ½ cup of the orange juice over medium heat for about 5 minutes. Stir well. Split the biscuits, spread with the melted jelly, and replace the tops. Place the biscuits, on their sides, in two columns in the buttered dish. Use as many as possible in the columns and then tuck the rest between the rows for a snug fit. Beat the eggs, milk, and sugar together, then add the scalded half-and-half in a slow but steady stream. Mix thoroughly. Strain the eggs onto the biscuits. Add as much as the pan will hold. The biscuits will try to float. Weight them down with another pan and some canned goods. Put in the refrigerator for up to 3 days.

Boil the leftover ½ cup of orange juice together with the other ½ cup of jam. Strain through a fine sieve. This will be one of the sauces for the pudding. The other will be crème anglaise (page 62).

Preheat the oven to 350° F. Remove the weight from the pudding and cover it tightly with buttered aluminum foil. Set the dish in the oven in a larger pan and add two inches of simmering water. This is the hard part. Sometimes this takes 1½ hours to cook; sometimes it takes twice that long. I don't know why. After an hour and a half, remove the foil. The pudding should have begun to firm up at least. If the egg has set, bake only long enough to make the top pretty and brown. If the center still appears to be gooey, continue checking at 20-minute intervals until the center feels firm and has puffed a little.

Serve the pudding warm with very cold crème anglaise and fresh whipped cream. Drizzle the raspberry sauce on top. The pudding reheats very well in the microwave.

SUMMER

B<small>Y SUMMER, AGRICULTURE</small> around here has gone wild. The late summer heat will eventually take its toll, but early on everything seems to grow. Everyone speculates on whether or not it will be a good tomato season, and people discuss which varieties they will be planting. Just when you are tired of the heavier dishes of cooler weather, the market provides dozens of fresh vegetables, herbs, and cheeses with which to make light meals.

My grandmothers and aunts cooked with the season because that was what was at hand. They used what was grown. Today the choice of things available locally is much larger. Fennel for example is a perfect early summer crop here, but it is fairly new to us. It is never mentioned in old recipes, but the cooks who wrote them would certainly have. I'm sure my grandmother would have. Southern cooking, like the South, has evolved. Traditions persist, but new ingredients and techniques have fueled change.

Tomato season here can be dismayingly short. People always seem to recall weeks and weeks of harvest, but often humidity and blight cut it down to just a week or two. Squash can go on and on. Zucchinis become baseball bats overnight, but eventually the stem borers will have their way. Lettuce never survives here beyond June. The heat comes down on it like a hammer. Summer herbs thrive through the season, as do peppers. People who have been clever have staggered their plantings of beans in hopes of an ongoing harvest.

Restaurant kitchens in this part of the world can be vile in late summer. Air conditioners are pointless. It is impossible to drink enough water. One defense is to switch to more cold or light dishes, and summer produce provides the perfect ingredients.

FRESH CHERRY SAUCE
FOR STRONG CHEESES

SOME YEARS BACK a friend returning from Italy brought me a present of rose petal marmalade. It was delicious but very strong flavored and quite distinct. I wasn't sure how to put it to its best use.

"They eat it on gorgonzola," she said.

"You're kidding?" I said. It was delicious.

The marmalade was soon gone, and although I had the recipe I never had time to find and harvest unsprayed roses when there were enough of them around. I devised this quick substitute to serve with the excellent cheeses produced here in Orange and Chatham Counties. Look for fresh farmhouse cheeses at your local farmers' market, the stronger the better. If these are not available, you too can use gorgonzola.

Makes about 1 quart

2 pounds of fresh cherries, unpitted with stems

½ cup sugar

3 tablespoons water

1 tablespoon rose flower water

⅛ teaspoon salt

Rinse the cherries and drain them in a colander, but don't dry them. (I am used to preserved cherries so I expect them to have seeds, but if you prefer, remove them. Try to keep the stems.) Roll them in the sugar. The sugar that clings to the wet cherries will be the right amount. Put the cherries in a non-reactive saucepan, add the water, cover, and cook on low heat. The cherries will soon (about 10 minutes) produce a great deal of bright red juice. Turn up the heat and reduce the liquid until it begins to appear syrupy, 5 or 6 minutes more. Remove from heat and add the rose flower water and the tiniest pinch of salt. Chill and serve as a side with a cheese plate.

This keeps well in the refrigerator. When the cherries are gone, you may use the remaining liquid as a substitute for water in your next batch. You can make this out of season, using store-bought frozen cherries. It will be good but will lack some of the appealing crunch.

WHITE PEACH AND PEPPER SOUP

I USE WHITE PEACHES for this soup but other kinds will work fine. The contrast of the sweetness of fruit with the piquance of pepper and bay is quite appealing.

Serves 4–6

2½ pounds white peaches

¼ cup sugar

1 cup inexpensive medium-sweet white wine

½ teaspoon dried red pepper flakes

2 teaspoons whole black peppercorns,
    tied up in cheesecloth or in a tea ball

2 bay leaves

1 cup half-and-half

Chopped fresh mint, for garnish

Peel and slice the peaches and toss with the sugar. Let them sit for 30 minutes and then pour them in a nonreactive pot with the wine and the seasonings. Bring them to a simmer until they are just heated through, about 2 minutes. If you go too far, they will turn a dull brown and taste like jelly. Fish out the bay leaves and the peppercorns and puree the soup. Add the half-and-half. Serve very cold with a garnish of chopped fresh mint. If the soup seems too thick, thin with a little more half-and-half.

BLUEBERRY SOUP

"I HAVE TASTED your blueberry soup. [pause] It is terrible." So pronounced one of my cooks, Luis Ortega, when I put this soup on the menu last summer. His objection was that the soup is not very sweet, but most people find this to be a pleasant surprise. It is another example of the unexpected refreshment that the combination of cold, spicy, and sweet can provide.

Serves 4–6

2 pints fresh blueberries

2 teaspoons whole black peppercorns,
    tied up in cheesecloth or a tea ball

2 bay leaves

3–3½ cups dry red wine

¼ cup heavy cream

2–4 tablespoons sugar (optional)

Sour cream and edible flowers, for garnish

Scald the blueberries, peppercorns, and bay leaves in 3 cups of the red wine until it just bubbles. You are only trying to cook the berries long enough to keep them from oxidizing. Let the soup cool slowly. Remove the peppercorns and bay leaves and puree the berries with a food mill or food processor. Add the heavy cream. Sometimes if the fruit is very tart, I add a little sugar, but I try not to be rash. This is not a smoothie. Some blueberries are juicier than others, so you may need to add more wine as well.

This soup is meant to be served cold, but it is also very good at room temperature. If it is around the Fourth of July, I garnish the soup with sour cream and bergamot flowers for a red, white, and blueberry effect. (This also works for Bastille Day.)

BAKED TOMATO SOUP

THIS IS WHAT you do that week in August when you suddenly have tons of ripe tomatoes.

Serves 4–6

5 pounds ripe tomatoes

8 cloves garlic, peeled

1 teaspoon salt

½ teaspoon freshly ground black pepper

1½ cup fresh basil, 1 cup whole leaves and ½ cup chiffonade

Juice and zest of 1 orange

Pinch of saffron (if the soup is to be hot)

1 cup plain yogurt (if the soup is to be cold)

Fresh popcorn

Cut away the stems and any blemishes from the tomatoes. Nestle them with the garlic in a nonreactive roasting pan with a tight-fitting lid. Sprinkle with the salt and pepper. Lay the whole basil leaves on top. Cover and bake at 350° F for about 2 hours until the tomatoes have completely collapsed and produced a great deal of juice. Stir in the orange juice and pick out any large basil stems. Puree the tomatoes with the juice, garlic, herbs, and all with a food mill, then stir in the basil chiffonade.

If the soup is to be served hot, add the saffron and orange zest and simmer for about 10 minutes over medium heat. If the soup is to be served cold, chill the puree and fold in the yogurt and orange zest. In either case, serve with fresh popcorn on the side.

GREEN PEACH SALAD

SOMETIMES YOU END up with unripe peaches despite your best efforts, especially if you buy a whole bushel. This is a wonderful way to use some of them. It is great with cold meats.

Serves 4–6

2½ pounds of unripe peaches, peeled and sliced as for a pie

Scant ¼ cup sugar

½ teaspoon salt

½ teaspoon freshly ground black pepper

2 tablespoons strong-flavored extra-virgin olive oil, like Greek or
    Lebanese

2 tablespoons fresh mint chiffonade

Toss the peaches with the sugar and the salt. Let them sit for 10 minutes. Fold in the pepper, oil, and mint. Serve cold within a few hours of preparation, as it will become mushy overnight.

MANGO SALAD

I GOT THIS IDEA at a festival that celebrates the cultures of all the Latin Americans who have settled here in North Carolina. (Don't miss these fiestas. The food is always fabulous. So is the music.) Several times a year, if you're lucky enough to have a Mexican grocery store in your town, you can suddenly get fragrant, luscious mangoes for about ten dollars a dozen.

Serves 4–6

4 mangoes of various ripeness

1 tablespoon extra-virgin olive oil

1 tablespoon chopped fresh mint

Juice of 1 lime

½ teaspoon sugar

⅛ teaspoon cayenne pepper plus more, for dusting

½ teaspoon salt

The salad is best if you have fruit of various degrees of ripeness. Peel them with sharp paring knife. After the mango is peeled, slice the flesh completely off of each side of the large flat seed in one big piece. Cut the fruit into large chunks and toss with the oil in a large bowl to keep them moist and separate, but don't make them greasy. Stir in the mint. Cover and chill for at least ½ hour.

When you are ready to serve the salad, douse it with the lime juice and stir in the sugar, salt, and cayenne. Arrange on a plate and dust the top with a little more cayenne. At the restaurant I use this as a first course, but at home I have used it as a dessert.

At the Latino festivals, the mangoes are left whole. They are peeled and scored with a knife and then stuck on a Popsicle stick, rolled in the lime juice, and dusted with the sugar, salt, and cayenne. (They are very messy.)

CUCUMBERS AND ONIONS

THIS IS A SIMPLE and essential summer recipe. It is good with everything and is a great addition to summer salad platters.

Serves 4–6

2½ pounds medium cucumbers

1 medium red onion, peeled, halved, and sliced

1 teaspoon salt

1 teaspoon whole celery seed

¼ cup apple cider vinegar

¼ cup extra-virgin olive oil

Wash the cucumbers. Those that are fresh from the garden are far superior to store-bought ones. I like to score the peels with a fork or zester. Cut the cucumbers into quarter inch rounds. Taste a slice of each cucumber because sometimes you get a very bitter one that can ruin the whole batch. Put the cukes and onion in a large mixing bowl and toss with the salt and the celery seed. Let them sit for 30 minutes to juice up. Then stir in the vinegar and oil. Taste for salt. Some people like to add pepper as well, but I can't decide. Serve cold.

TOMATO AND WATERMELON SALAD

MANY RECIPES HAVE resulted from the sudden wave of produce that begins arriving in midsummer. Tomato soups and sauces, pickles and relishes, lavish *salades composées*. In mid-August, I often have tomatoes or melons on several dishes at once and fresh herbs show up everywhere. This salad is a new discovery thanks to the fact that I sometimes don't pay attention when I am ordering.

Serves 4–6

5 cups ripe, bite-sized watermelon chunks, seeded as best you can, but
    don't go crazy

1½ pounds very ripe tomatoes, finely chunked

3 teaspoons sugar

½ teaspoon salt

1 small red onion, peeled, quartered, and thinly sliced

½ cup red wine vinegar

¼ cup good, strong-flavored extra-virgin olive oil

    Toss the melon and tomatoes with the sugar and salt. Let sit for 15 minutes. Then fold in the onions, vinegar, and oil. Serve very cold. This salad is amazingly refreshing.

SALADES COMPOSÉES

MOST NICE RESTAURANTS like to have a salad that is a notch up from the basic green one. These composed salads have a million forms and you can use anything you have in them. I use them year-round and simply change the name as the seasons progress. I've suggested a few ingredients here that I use for their colors as well as flavors. You can prepare individual plates or, better yet, a big colorful platter that can be passed around the table.

WARM SALAD WITH GOAT CHEESE

Serves 6

2 medium red beets

2 medium yellow beets

3–4 small blue potatoes

3 small leeks, trimmed and soaked in cold water

3 tablespoons extra-virgin olive oil

½ teaspoon salt

2 tablespoons chopped fresh herbs, such as thyme, basil, and Italian
    flat-leaf parsley

1 pound mixed salad greens

1 5½-ounce log of fresh chèvre-style goat cheese

Sherry Vinaigrette (page 160)

Any other saladlike items you may have around, such as
    Roasted Peppers with Mustard and Anchovies (page 159)
    or the Romano Beans with Oil and Sea Salt (page 159)

You must steam each vegetable separately, as each one has a different cooking time, even the different-colored beets. Beets will stain anything cooked with them anyway. You never know how long it will take beets to cook, so make sure that the steamer is filled with as much water as possible. Place them in the boiling steamer and check them after 20 minutes. A paring knife should pass easily all the way to the center. Keep checking every 10 minutes until this happens. Cool the beets in ice water. Red beets will need their own water bath. Everything else can be cooled together.

Small potatoes will take 10–15 minutes. The knife should pierce them in the same way. Leeks take 8–10 minutes. They are stringy, so it is important that they be done through. Again, pierce with the knife. After they have been put in ice water, examine them for sand. I usually slide off the outer layer or two to make sure they are not gritty. Cut them into inch-long pieces.

As you finish preparing the vegetables, keep them separate from one another. Peel the beets by rubbing them with a dish towel; the peel should come right off. Sometimes I like to cut them into large dice, sometimes into rounds. In any case, moisten them with a little olive oil and toss with the salt and chopped herbs.

Some potatoes have nice peels and some don't. Decide whether you prefer them peeled or not. Slice the potatoes into quarter-inch-thick rounds.

Preheat the oven to 350° F (or use your toaster oven). Arrange all the vegetables in an attractive way on top of nice salad greens. I like to put small separate clumps of each item to accentuate the different colors.

Put the discs of goat cheese on an oiled baking sheet and warm them in the oven. Carefully slide them on top of the salad. They will be soft when warm. Dress with warmed Sherry Vinaigrette with pumpkin seeds. Decorate with the roasted peppers and Romano beans. Serve at once.

ROASTED PEPPERS WITH MUSTARD AND ANCHOVIES

Makes about 1½ cups

2 anchovy fillets or 2 teaspoons anchovy paste

1 tablespoon Dijon mustard

1 tablespoon extra-virgin olive oil

2 large red, yellow, and/or orange bell peppers, roasted, peeled, cored, seeded, and cut into strips

1 teaspoon drained capers

2 teaspoons chopped Italian flat-leaf parsley

Mash the anchovies and mustard together with a fork in a medium bowl to form a paste. Whisk in the oil to form an emulsion. Add the pepper strips, capers, and parsley, and toss to coat. Chill. Use as a part of a *salade composée.*

ROMANO BEANS WITH OIL AND SEA SALT

Romano beans are a variety of pole bean that is delicious when eaten raw. Many other vegetables are delicious when prepared this way. I have used baby asparagus, green beans, snow peas, and sugar snaps.

Makes about ½ pound

½ pound of fresh, washed, trimmed Romano beans

1 teaspoon coarse sea salt

2 tablespoons extra-virgin olive oil

Toss everything together and use in a *salade composeé*

SHERRY VINAIGRETTE

Makes about 1 cup

¼ cup sherry vinegar

1 teaspoon salt

¼ teaspoon sugar

1 teaspoon Dijon mustard

1 small shallot, peeled and chopped (about 1 tablespoon)

1 small clove garlic, peeled and minced

¾ cup extra-virgin olive oil

1 tablespoon unsalted butter

½ cup raw hulled pumpkin seeds

¼ teaspoon salt

Mix the vinegar, salt, sugar, mustard, shallot, and garlic together in a small bowl. Whisk in the oil to make an emulsion. Gently warm in a saucepan or the microwave and then add the pumpkin seeds (below) just before dressing the salad.

Melt the butter in a small skillet. When it begins to bubble, add the pumpkin seeds and toss until they begin to pop like popcorn, 3–4 minutes. Add the salt and toss to coat.

COLLARDS

HARDLY A WORKDAY passes that I don't eat at least a spoonful of collards. I never grow tired of them. I also love to drink their broth and to pour the broth over rice. My great-grandmother used to say that this "pot liquor" was like medicine. She also said that eating collards was how poor people survived the Depression, because collards will grow almost anywhere under almost any conditions and are very nourishing. People would plant them in their yards back then, and they still do. Essentially all you do to collards is boil them for a long time with salt. At Crook's I almost always have a ham bone to add. Most butcher shops and meat departments will have some sort of ham bone or ham hocks for sale.

Serves 4–6

2 bunches (about 5 pounds) fresh collards

6 strips of bacon, diced

1 large onion, peeled and diced

1 teaspoon dried red pepper flakes

2 teaspoons salt

1 ham bone

Remove the tougher, woody stalks from the collard leaves. Smaller stems are okay. Wash the leaves and cut them into half-inch-wide strips. You can roll them into cigars to speed this up.

Put the bacon in a stock pot on high heat to render its grease, 3 or so minutes. Add the onion and cook until translucent but not brown, about 5 minutes more. Add the collards and cover with cool water. Add the red pepper, salt, and the ham bone. Bring to a boil and cook for at least 2 hours. There are many conflicting opinions on this. To my mind, collards were not made for quick cooking. Undercook collards and you are asking to be strangled; they can't be properly chewed. On the other hand, overcook them and they will eventually turn to mush. Two hours seems about right, although this might give nutritionists pause. Taste for salt.

Even people who love collards complain about the way they make the house smell while cooking. People have different cures for this: Place four pecans in the pot. Cover the top of the collards with slices of white bread. None of this works.

Rockers in the Kitchen

Chapel Hill is an important music city. It has great radio and a collection of sturdy music clubs. This scene will almost allow a musician to live by his art. A shift or two in a bar or restaurant kitchen is often all that is needed for a modest lifestyle.

For a while, between the Vietnamese and Mexicans, I had rockers and their entourages. These were guys, mostly, who were in or hung around local bands, needed flexible schedules, and lived by the creed of work hard, play hard. Their bands were innovative and often short-lived. Sometimes I would get a CD or two before they disbanded.

These people were generally very smart and, except for the occasional hangover, seldom any trouble. Sometimes they had outrageous clothes and hair, but more often they were just sort of rough-and-tumble young guys. They were poets, but like as not they didn't think of themselves in those terms. The poetry showed up in their work, though. Once I persuaded them that their job was worth doing well, they pursued it with all seriousness. Unlike foodies, they rarely panicked under kitchen duress. They just bore down and dug in. They seldom came to the job with sophisticated food backgrounds, but they were adventurous and fearless, and this made them able to absorb the new information quickly. As soon as I left the kitchen, they'd change the radio from NPR to loud driving music, to which they danced around and lip-synced between cooking dinner runs.

This made for heady nights. Great music was always in town, often right across the street, and it was just getting started when we all got off work. I'm too old to carry on like that now, but I remember it fondly. "No tears for the creatures of the night."

FIGS WITH HAM AND SAUCE BELLEVUE

I DON'T REMEMBER where the recipe for this sauce came from, but in the depths of my memory I associate it with poached fish. These days, however, I use it on the wonderful fresh figs that I get each summer from Mrs. Andrews. The turkey fig, the indigenous one in North Carolina, has two harvests here. In midsummer you get a small first harvest of fruit that was set in late fall. About a month later comes a much larger crop that is set in the spring. By all accounts this is the perfect first course.

Serves 4–6

SAUCE BELLEVUE

1 tablespoon finely chopped fresh mint

¼ cup of white wine vinegar

2 tablespoons sour cream

1½ tablespoons Dijon mustard

1½ tablespoons sugar

½–⅔ cup extra-virgin olive oil

12 fresh figs

2 ounces country ham (or prosciutto if you can't find any), sliced tissue thin

⅛ teaspoon sugar mixed with a pinch of salt

To make the sauce: Macerate the mint in the vinegar and set aside for 10 minutes to develop the flavor. Meanwhile mix together the sour cream, mustard, and sugar. Whisk the vinegar and mint into this and then gradually whisk in the oil drop by drop until you have a thick emulsion. You may not need all of the oil. Then again, you may need a drop or two more. Emulsification can be treacherous.

You will have about a cup of sauce, which is enough for many figs. Cut the figs in half. Dust with a tiny, tiny amount of the sugar-salt mixture. Drape a little country ham over each fig half and then a bit of the sauce. Serve at room temperature.

PORK ROAST WITH ARTICHOKE STUFFING

THIS ROAST CAN be a main course for a cold summer supper. It can be thinly sliced and put out with cold cuts and pâtés on an appetizer platter. It is also excellent when eaten with the hands while standing in front of an open refrigerator.

The filling is a sort of 1950s country-club food, the kind of stuff that is really good but that we're not supposed to like because it contains a box of pudding mix or a package of frozen peas. It came out of a search for hors d'oeuvres for a vegetarian birthday party before I realized that Worchestershire sauce contains anchovies. It is great as a spread for garlic toast or crackers. I have abandoned using it as a spread and have switched to using it as a stuffing for a roast pork loin that is going to be served cold. This is a hybrid of many Junior League cookbook recipes, as evidenced by the abundance of brand names.

Serves 4–6 generously

1 center-cut boneless pork loin (3–4 pounds)
Artichoke Heart Stuffing (page 167)
2 teaspoons salt
1 teaspoon freshly ground black pepper
2 tablespoons vegetable oil

Preheat oven to 350° F. Remove the string (or netting) from the roast and let it fall into two halves. Insert a long, thin, sharp knife lengthwise all the way through the center of one piece of the roast. Use the handle of a long wooden spoon (or your fingers) to widen the slit into a 2-inch-wide tunnel. Fill the tunnel with the artichoke stuffing from both ends of the roast. Truss the filled loin tightly with kitchen twine at 3-inch intervals to make it as cylindrical as possible. Repeat, cutting, stuffing, and tying the other half of the roast.

Salt and pepper the outside of both pieces and brown all over in the vegetable oil in a large skillet. Roast on a rack in the oven until the center reads 150° F on a thermometer, 35–40 minutes.

Allow to cool completely. Remove the string before slicing.

ARTICHOKE HEART STUFFING

Makes enough for one pork roast

1 13¾-ounce can of artichoke hearts, drained

¼ cup Hellmann's mayonnaise

10 Ritz crackers, coarsely crushed

½ cup freshly grated Parmesan cheese

½ teaspoon freshly squeezed lemon juice

¼ teaspoon Worcestershire sauce

Mash together with a fork the artichoke hearts and the mayonnaise. Fold in the crackers and Parmesan cheese, and season with the lemon juice and Worchestershire sauce.

MILLIONAIRES' CHICKEN

I FIRST HAD this salad years ago. My friend Elizabeth Brown is a wonderful cook and she would bring this to potlucks. I have lost track of Elizabeth, unfortunately, so I have tried to re-create this from memory. Hers was prettier, but this tastes the same, as best as I can remember. I once asked her about the name and she said it was called Millionaires' Chicken because it was good enough for— who else?—millionaires.

Serves 4–6

1 tablespoon peeled, grated fresh ginger

1 tablespoon (packed) brown sugar

2 tablespoons mushroom soy sauce

½ cup sesame oil

1 teaspoon peanut oil

1 scallion (white and green parts), trimmed and chopped

3½ cups meat from 1 velvetized chicken (see page 15)

1 head romaine lettuce, washed and sliced across the leaves
    as for Caesar salad

2 tablespoons toasted sesame seeds

1 small can chow mein noodles

Mix the ginger, brown sugar, and soy sauce together. Let sit for 10 minutes. Whisk the sesame and peanut oils together and then whisk these into the soy sauce mixture as if you were making vinaigrette. Strain out the ginger fibers (you will need to mash the sauce with a fork to extract it all). Toss the chicken with the sauce, drain a bit, and then toss with the scallions. Arrange on the romaine lettuce on a serving plate and sprinkle with the sesame seeds and the noodles.

I also use this recipe as one component of a summer cold plate that might also include Tomato and Watermelon Salad (page 156), Cucumbers and Onions (page 155), Green Peach Salad (page 153), or sliced summer tomatoes.

COLD FRIED CHICKEN

OBVIOUSLY, THIS STARTS out as hot fried chicken and can be eaten as such, but I've always thought that one of life's great blessings is discovering a big pile of yesterday's fried chicken in the refrigerator. Self-rising flour and buttermilk combine to make a thick, fluffy crust. I have no use for people who whine about breading on fried foods.

Serves 4

½ cup salt

1 gallon water

1 whole chicken (about 3 pounds) cut up into 8 pieces

1 cup buttermilk

1 cup self-rising flour

1 teaspoon salt

1 teaspoon freshly ground black pepper

Vegetable oil for frying, enough to fill your skillet to ½ inch

Boil the salt with 1 quart of the water to dissolve it and then add it back into rest of the water you will need. Make enough to submerge the amount of chicken you will fry. Cover the chicken pieces with the brine, weight down with a plate, and refrigerate overnight.

The next day drain and pat dry the chicken. Coat the pieces with the buttermilk. Heat the oil on high heat in a dutch oven until is very hot but not smoking. If you have a thermometer, the temperature should register 360° F.

If you don't have a thermometer, when the oil begins to shimmer, sprinkle a little flour over it. If it sizzles furiously, it's probably ready. Make a dredge of the flour, salt, and pepper. Piece by piece, after the oil is already hot, shake off the buttermilk, roll the chicken in the flour, and shake off the excess again.

Fry only as much chicken as you can without crowding it. Chicken breasts cook more quickly than the legs and thighs, so I try to cook them in like batches. When the first side is browned (5–8 minutes), turn each piece, reduce the heat to medium, and cover. Cook till done through, about 12 minutes for the breasts and 20 minutes for thighs and larger pieces, checking often to avoid burning. The exact times will vary, of course, according to the size of the pieces. Uncover for the last few minutes to recrisp the crust. Drain the chicken as it is done. Pick at the crust early on to see if it is salty enough. Let the oil return to 360° F for each new batch. If you are frying a whole lot of chicken, you may need to change the oil if it becomes full of burned flour.

Transfer the chicken to a baking rack set over a cookie sheet to drain. Let it cool uncovered to room temperature and then refrigerate uncovered. Serve with Cucumbers and Onions (page 155), Potato Salad (page 121), or Tomato and Watermelon Salad (page 156).

BOURBON BROWN SAUCE
FOR GRILLED STEAKS AND SAUTÉED
CHICKEN LIVERS

AT CROOK'S CORNER we use this sauce on almost all of our steaks, even if we are going to put something else on top like herb butter or Jerusalem Artichoke Relish (page 18). An excellent way to finish cooking a steak is to simmer it carefully in a little of the sauce for a few minutes. Then remove the meat and reduce the sauce to thicken it, swirl in a little butter until completely absorbed and pour it over the steak.

This recipe makes enough sauce for four to six steaks, but to me it makes more sense to make it in large batches and then reduce it down and freeze it in small batches for later use. Besides, it is hard to make a small amount of brown stock.

Makes about 6 cups

2 large shallots, peeled and coarsely chopped

2 cups dry red wine

⅓ cup red wine vinegar

4 cups Brown Stock (page 13)

½ cup of heavy cream

¼ cup of bourbon

Put the shallots into a large pot with 1 cup of the wine and the vinegar. Turn the heat to high and reduce to a syrupy consistency, about 10 minutes. This is very easy to burn, so don't wander off. Do not allow the shallots to brown at all. When the wine is reduced, add the stock. Reduce by two-thirds. Add the heavy cream. Reduce by one-half and add the rest of the wine. Reduce back down to the original level. Add the bourbon and return the sauce to a boil, but do not reduce. Strain. This sauce can be used at once, stored in the refrigerator, or frozen.

This sauce will keep refrigerated for one month, but sometimes the cream will layer out to the top. Just stir it back together before use. It will be very thick when cold.

If you have very little of this sauce left (1 cup or less) you can carefully reduce it to an even thicker syrup, cool it a little, and then beat it into a pound of softened butter. Called wine merchants' butter, this is delicious on steak or on toast.

FRESH TOMATO PASTA

THIS IS SOMETHING that I make every summer, at the restaurant and at home, when there is a sudden flood of fresh tomatoes and I need to use them lavishly and fast. You can use any kind of pasta, but I am partial to the really fat spaghetti.

Serves 4–6

2½ pounds really ripe tomatoes (different varieties if you have them)

4 tablespoons (½ stick) unsalted butter

1 generous tablespoon chopped garlic

1 pound spaghetti

1 teaspoon salt

½ teaspoon pepper

Freshly grated Parmesan cheese

Cook the spaghetti according to the instructions on the package. Wash the tomatoes and trim away the stem ends and any blemishes. Rough cut them into largish chunks. In a large skillet melt the butter. When it starts to foam, add the garlic. When this starts to smell good, but before the garlic has begun to brown (30 seconds), add the tomatoes and cook them until they just start to collapse, 2 minutes max. Add the pasta and stir quickly to heat. Season with the salt and pepper. Serve at once. Offer the cheese for people to sprinkle on top. This is a quick and delicious supper, especially if you have one or two tomato plants outside the back door.

FRESH TOMATO TART

THIS RECIPE, like so many others, was born of the constant torment provided by being forced to come up with vegetarian main courses on an otherwise sensible menu. I have to admit that this *is* very good, especially when the tomatoes are ripe and you have all kinds and colors. It is very important to have all the ingredients assembled and prepared before you start to cook the cornmeal. It will set up quickly once you begin and you will not have time to stop and prepare more of anything.

Serves 4–6

4–6 ripe tomatoes, sliced as for a sandwich but cut in half
   if the tomatoes are really large

½ cup rinsed, large-curd whole-fat cottage cheese, drained

2 large eggs, beaten

3 tablespoons chopped fresh summer herbs
   (such as basil or marjoram)

3 cups water

1½ teaspoons salt

1 cup plain yellow or white cornmeal

2 tablespoons softened unsalted butter

½ cup grated Cheddar cheese

1 small red onion, peeled and diced

½ teaspoon freshly ground black pepper

½ cup freshly grated Parmesan cheese

1 cup sour cream

Preheat the oven to 350° F. Butter an 11-inch tart pan with a removable bottom and set aside. Make sure you have enough tomatoes to completely cover the top like the rings of fruit on a French dessert tart.

Place the cottage cheese in a fine sieve and gently rinse under cool water. Set aside to drain. Whisk the eggs and 2 tablespoons of the herbs together well in a bowl and set aside.

Bring 1½ cups of the water to a boil in a large heavy-bottomed pot. Add ½ teaspoon of the salt. Once boiling, quickly whisk the cornmeal and remaining 1½ cups of water together, then into the boiling pot. Stir without ceasing with a wooden spoon until the cornmeal pulls away from the sides of the pot in large, dry-looking bubbles. Sometimes this happens quickly and sometimes it doesn't. The cornmeal is ready when when you can tip the pan and have most of the mixture pull away dry.

Quickly stir in the butter until it is completely absorbed. Add the eggs all at once and stir rapidly so that they don't become scrambled eggs. Next add the Cheddar cheese, followed by the onion (you want it to remain crunchy), and the cottage cheese (you don't want it to melt away). Stir only long enough to combine. Quickly pour this mixture into the tart pan and spread it to the edges with a buttered teacup so you don't burn your fingers. (Your wooden spoon will work okay for this, but the cornmeal will stick to it more.) You may have more than you need. The volume of this stuff varies mysteriously.

The cornmeal will begin to set at once, so quickly begin to layer in the slices of tomatoes, starting from the outside of the pan, in concentric circles like the rings of fruit on a French dessert tart. Dig the bottom of each slice into the cornmeal a little. This will cause the tart to thicken as you move toward the center. That's okay. The rings of tomato slices should overlap a little.

Sprinkle with the rest of the salt and the pepper and bake for 30 minutes. The tart may look a little wet at this point but it will set up as it bakes. Sprinkle with the Parmesan cheese and bake another 15 minutes until the cheese is a little brown and crispy. Let rest for 10 minutes before unmolding and slicing. Mix the sour cream with the remaining herbs. Serve warm. This reheats beautifully.

SKILLET EGGPLANT

THIS RECIPE WAS given to me by a friend of a friend at a covered-dish dinner years ago and I promptly lost it. Then, miraculously, it fluttered unaltered out of an old notebook when I was looking for something else. I use this as a main course, but it would be a great addition to one of those summer buffet suppers when "we're eating out of the garden tonight."

When I tasted this at the party, I complimented the cook who told me that it was a dish that his grandmother made often. When I asked if his grandmother was an Italian, he replied, "No, she's an old lady from Asheville."

Serves 4–6

2 pounds eggplant, peeled and cut into 1-inch cubes (about 6 cups)

1½ teaspoons salt

1 medium onion, peeled and cut into large dice (about 1 cup)

¼ cup extra-virgin olive oil

1½ tablespoons (packed) light brown sugar

¼ cup balsamic or sherry vinegar

½–1 cup water

¾ cup large stuffed green olives, drained

½ teaspoon freshly ground black pepper

1 cup feta cheese, coarsely crumbled, or
   a ball of fresh mozzarella, cubed

Dust the eggplant with salt and place in a colander to sweat for 20 minutes. Sauté the onion in a large skillet in oil until it begins to soften and brown slightly. Shake off the eggplant and add to the onion, in batches if necessary, as it cooks down. Don't worry about the salt. Add the brown sugar, then the vinegar, and then enough water (start with ½ cup) to lubricate the stew. Cover and simmer for 15 minutes. Stir in the olives and warm through, about 3 minutes. Add the pepper and, if necessary, the rest of the salt. Lastly, fold in the cheese. After you have made this once, you may want to adjust the amounts of sugar or vinegar to match your idea of sweet and sour.

WILD MUSHROOM PASTA

Every summer, if conditions are right, Mary Ayres brings me fresh wild mushrooms—usually black trumpets or chanterelles—that she finds while surveying land. Because of their fragility, they cannot be washed, so I break off the lower part of each stem and then blow on each mushroom to remove as much dirt as possible. The stems are always very sandy so I simmer them in the heavy cream to extract their flavor. The strained cream will be used in the sauce. If you don't have access to wild mushrooms, you may substitute store-bought exotic varieties such as porcini, sliced into thin strips.

Serves 4–6

4 cups fettuccini

1 pound wild mushrooms

2 cups heavy cream

3 tablespoons unsalted butter

½ teaspoon chopped garlic

2 tablespoons Madeira

1 teaspoon salt

½ teaspoon freshly ground black pepper

½ cup finely sliced scallions (white and green parts)

Cook the fettuccini according to the instructions on the package. Drain well and keep at room temperature. Examine the mushrooms. Trumpets are far too fragile to wash so you must dry-clean them. Blow on each one as you break off the stems by hand (or you can try using a soft cloth or a pastry brush instead). Simmer the stems in the cream over low heat for 20 minutes or so until it is reduced to 1½ cups. Don't let the cream come to a hard boil. Strain the cream through a fine sieve. If you don't have one that seems fine enough, use a coffee filter, but this will be very slow.

In a heavy skillet melt the butter over medium-high heat and add the garlic. When the butter begins to sizzle, add the mushrooms. Do not let the garlic or the mushrooms brown. Toss the pan until mushrooms begin to wilt (about 3 minutes) and then hit it with the Madeira—it may flare up—and then the reduced, strained cream. Cook quickly over high heat until the cream looks thick and lustrous. This happens fast—no longer than 5 minutes—so be careful. Add the salt, pepper, and scallions. Stir in the precooked fettuccini and toss to coat. Check the seasoning and serve at once. Don't add any cheese; it tends to overpower the flavor of the mushrooms.

BASIC VANILLA ICE CREAM
WITH VARIATIONS

THE VARIETIES OF ice cream are endless. This recipe can be the starting point for many other flavors. I am always being surprised by new ones. A friend once returned from Stockholm with reports of one called salty licorice. It sounded like medicine but was delicious (if you like licorice). Another time Hong, my Vietnamese friend, brought in frozen durian pulp. The result was an ice cream that made you think that perhaps you had, well, stepped in something. It is apparently forbidden to bring fresh durians into hotels in Singapore because of this odor. These recipes are all much tamer.

Makes 1½ quarts

8 large egg yolks

¾ cup sugar

1¾ cups half-and-half

1 split vanilla bean

6 tablespoons (¾ stick) unsalted butter

1½ cups heavy cream

Separate the eggs. You will use the yolks only, but you might want to save the whites for another purpose. Whisk the sugar into the egg yolks and set aside.

Scald the half-and-half with the vanilla bean. When it is hot but not boiling, whisk it into the egg yolks in a thin stream. Put the mixture into the top of a double boiler and stir constantly until it begins to thicken and give off a faint steam from its surface, about 10 minutes. The custard should coat the back of a spoon. Be careful not to overcook or you will get scrambled eggs. Lower the heat and stir in a little of the butter. Remove from heat and stir in the rest of the butter bit by small bit. Be sure that the butter is completely absorbed. Uncombined lumps will turn into pockets of grease. Add the cream and strain. Chill the custard in the refrigerator (or over ice if you are in a hurry). Churn in an ice-cream maker.

Some people are startled by the amount of butter, cream, and eggs in this, but if you only eat the occasional bowl you'll be fine. This ice cream is delicious by itself but of course can be embellished with chocolate sauce or fruit or put into a float or soda.

COFFEE ICE CREAM

Add 1 tablespoon of good-quality instant coffee to the scalding half-and-half. After the ice cream is churned, stir in 1 teaspoon of ground coffee.

CHERRY VANILLA ICE CREAM

Add ¼ cup of dried cherries to the scalding half-and-half. Let steep for 30 minutes. Reheat the half-and-half and proceed with the original recipe.

PRALINE ICE CREAM

Stir in ¼ cup of Nutella and ½ cup of Candied Pecans (page 180) into the vanilla ice cream when it comes out of the churn.

CANDIED PECANS

2 cups coarsely chopped pecan pieces, sifted well in a colander

1 cup plus a bit more sugar

2 teaspoons salt

Put a heavy skillet on high heat. When it is warm, add the sifted pecans. (Crumbs will burn up before you finish.) Heat the nuts alone for a minute, stirring them constantly with a wooden spoon. Sprinkle ½ cup of the sugar over the nuts. Continue stirring. At this point you really need to keep things moving because this burns easily. The sugar will begin to melt. Add the salt. Keep stirring and add the remaining ½ cup of sugar. Stir only to coat the nuts and turn out onto a cool baking sheet. Move them apart to prevent from clumping. When they have cooled a bit, toss them in a little more sugar. Obviously, the nuts must be cold before they are added to ice cream.

FRESH FIG ICE CREAM

Stem ½ pound of fresh figs and split them in half lengthwise. Toss them in 2 tablespoons of sugar. Let this juice for half an hour.

Simmer this mixture, together with 2 tablespoons of water in a large frying pan for about 2 minutes, just until the figs begin to turn bright red. They should barely begin to steam. Mash them up a bit with a fork to break up any large clumps that would freeze hard. Cool the figs and fold into the vanilla ice cream when it comes out of the churn.

BUTTER PECAN ICE CREAM

Sift ½ cup of pecan pieces. Put 3 tablespoons of whole butter in a skillet. Turn the heat to high. As soon as the butter begins to melt, add the nuts and ⅛ teaspoon of salt. Swirl the pan constantly until the butter begins to brown and smells toasty. Immediately pour the nuts and butter into a metal bowl that is sitting in ice and stir until cool. Fold this into the vanilla ice cream base and churn.

REALLY GOOD BANANA PUDDING

APPARENTLY, I CAN'T be allowed to publish a cookbook that doesn't contain this recipe. I resisted including it because the component that makes it exceptional, the pastry cream, is not my own invention, but borrowed. That being said, this is one of the things that, by popular demand, I almost always have on the menu.

Banana pudding has been around forever, and most people use the recipe on the box of vanilla wafers, but for some reason I can never quite ignore the taste of raw flour in the custard, and I've always disliked it. I often have to teach dessert cooks, and these days that can mean simplifying things and translating them into another language. Years ago I converted all the measurements, liquid and dry, so that they all could be done with the same beat-up clear plastic measuring cups that I have in my kitchen. The distinction between the two makes no sense to Mexican teenagers raised on metrics. And I work from a stained spiral notebook that I put together with Francisco Guzman years ago wherein all the titles are in English and all the instructions and ingredients are in Spanish. To achieve these goals I often refer to the pie and cake "bibles" published in the late 1980s by Rose Levy Beranbaum. She gives clear and concise instructions for all the basics. I only have to alter them for restaurant volumes and conditions.

While I was teaching Francisco how to make this pudding, I came across Beranbaum's alternative recipe for pastry cream that uses cornstarch instead of flour. We decided to experiment and the results were deluxe. I make mine runnier than she recommends, and I think I incorporate more butter at the end, but credit must be given where credit is due.

People love this. The custard absorbs the flavor of the bananas and properly sogs out the cookies. Magically, the cornstarch keeps the bananas from blackening.

I cook the meringue separately so I can cool the pudding quickly, but at home you may brown it on top in the traditional manner.

Serves 10 plus

4 cups half-and-half

1 vanilla bean

6 tablespoons cornstarch

4 large eggs

1 cup sugar

8 tablespoons (1 stick), unsalted butter

1 box natural vanilla wafers

2½ pounds ripe bananas

Meringue (page 184)

Scald 6½ cups of the half-and-half with the split vanilla bean in a heavy-bottomed pot until it just steams and begins to form a skin, about 5 minutes over medium-high heat. Do not boil. Meanwhile, beat the cornstarch into the remaining 1½ cups of half-and-half to dissolve it. Then beat in the eggs. Whisk the hot half-and-half into the egg mixture in a slow stream. Strain all this back into the heavy-bottomed pot. Return the vanilla bean. Cook over medium-high heat, stirring constantly. In 3–5 minutes, the custard will begin to thicken and to tug at the whisk. Continue to stir for a few minutes more, being sure to move the whisk over the entire bottom of the pot. When the surface begins to steam a little, gradually stir in the sugar. Be careful, because this will make the custard more likely to burn on the bottom. Remove from the heat and beat in the butter 2 tablespoons at a time. Stir constantly so that the butter is absorbed before it separates. This will temporarily thin the custard. Discard the vanilla beans.

Pour a cup of the hot custard into an 8 × 10 × 3 casserole dish. Line the bottom and sides with vanilla wafers. (I always use Nabisco Nilla Wafers. Do not buy the artificially flavored ones. You can really tell the difference.) Slice the bananas over the cookies, then layer any remaining cookies over the bananas. Gently fill the casserole with the rest of the custard.

MERINGUE

Makes enough for 1 pudding

2 tablespoons cider vinegar

¼ teaspoon salt

¾ cup egg whites (from about 8 large eggs)

¼ teaspoon cream of tartar

1 cup sugar

While the pudding is settling, prepare the meringue. Put the vinegar and salt in a mixing bowl. Swirl the bowl around and dump it out over the sink. The vinegar and salt that clings to the bowl will be the right amount. Add the egg whites and begin beating with a mixer at medium speed. Add the cream of tartar. Increase the mixer speed a bit, and drizzle in ¾ cup of the sugar. When the sugar is absorbed, increase the speed to high and beat until stiff peaks form.

Spread the meringue over the top of the pudding with a spatula, making lots of dramatic swirls and curlicues. Sprinkle the rest of the sugar evenly over the top. Bake for 30 minutes at 300°F, checking from time to time for browning. When it begins to color, turn up the heat to 325°F and cook for 10 minutes more or until the points are toasty. Serve hot, warm, or cold—this can be served at once or day-old.

EPILOGUE
Quebec 2005

I AM OFTEN ASKED to list the ingredients of a perfect meal or perhaps to recall a perfect dinner party. The first thing on the list is always the same: good companions. Some people are skeptical of this answer, but I invite you to choose between a delicious dinner with unpleasant company and a package of Nabs and two Pepsis with your best friend in the waiting room of a train station.

If you can combine good friends with a good dinner, you are very lucky indeed. Then the magic of the table can really kick in. Good wine, the faces of friends aglow in the candlelight, animated conversation, and laughter becoming louder. Such evenings are perfect. I have heard that the Romans have a saying that one doesn't age at the table. I believe that one might actually grow younger, if only for a while.

I am in Quebec City tonight, far from the South. I often come here to both relax and to work. I find that I need to get out of town to do either—my profession is so demanding. I have done a lot of the writing of this book here in fact. The distance seems to help me focus and the distractions are seldom serious. I am sitting at my favorite restaurant, the Café St. Malo on the rue Saint Paul. I have had a pastis and now Yolande has brought me a broiled veal kidney with port sauce. Its accompaniment is a plate of French fries with mayonnaise—yes, mayonnaise, and nothing more. Life can be so good.

ACKNOWLEDGMENTS

Thanks are due to many, but here are a few most directly pertinent to this book.
To Gene Hamer for telling me to write it; to Paul Covington for allowing me the time
to write; to Maxine Mills and Anne Winslow for a lovely design; to Moreton Neal
for teaching me style; to Cheri Klein for teaching me a certain useful daring;
to Rick Robinson for his remarkable archives; to Katharine Walton for nudging me on;
to Sheri Castle for testing the recipes; and to Kathy Pories for editing them.

INDEX